BLACK VENUS

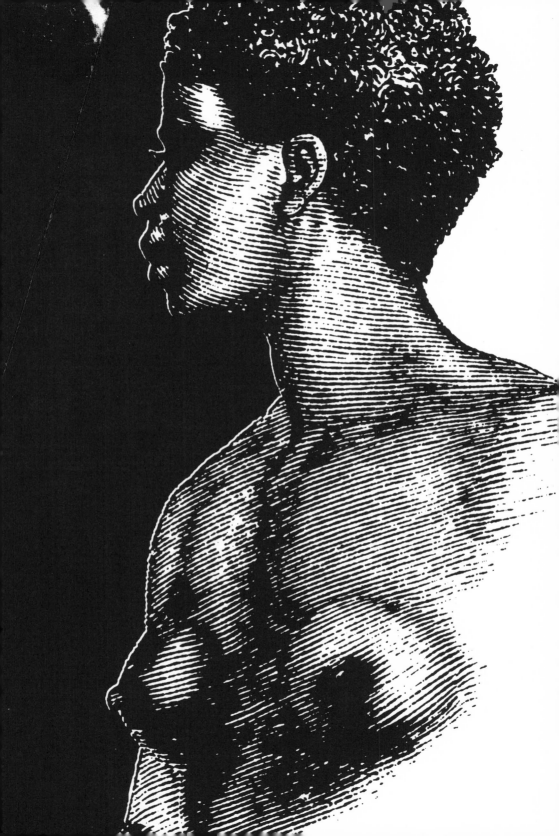

BLACK VENUS

Sexualized Savages,

Primal Fears, and

Primitive Narratives

in French

T. Denean Sharpley-Whiting

Duke University Press

1999

© 1999 Duke University Press
All rights reserved
Printed in the United States of America
on acid-free paper ⊛
Designed by C. H. Westmoreland
Typeset in Monotype Fournier with Gill Sans
display by Tseng Information Systems, Inc.
Library of Congress Cataloging-in-Publication
Data appear on the last printed page
of this book.

For my grandmother,

Bertalorina Mae Webb,

1910–1997

CONTENTS

ILLUSTRATIONS

ACKNOWLEDGMENTS

There are a number of people who have been a tremendous help with this work. I would like to thank first and foremost my reviewers and Sharon Parks-Torian, senior editorial assistant at Duke University Press, for all their support, encouragement, and tenacity. This manuscript is what it is because of them. I can't begin to thank them for rereading the manuscript each time (three times to be precise) I decided to add another chapter.

The enthusiasm and support of Reynolds Smith, executive editor at Duke University Press, are catching. I greatly appreciate the leads on the "Hottentot Apron."

Georges Van Den Abbeele has believed in this project from its rather ambitious beginnings. I have valued his mentoring through the years. Edward J. Ahearn, my dissertation director at Brown University, has always been there to generously give advice and much needed support. I am grateful to Françoise Lionnet for the suggestions regarding Baudelaire. I thank Robert Bernasconi, Thadious Davis, Christopher Dunn, Michael E. Dyson, Karen Fields, Joy James, Valerie Orlando, Nell Painter, Tiffany Patterson, Marjorie Salvodon, Brother Yonah Seleti, and (during fall 1997) the people at Princeton University's Shelby Cullom Davis Center for their feedback. I would also like to thank my colleagues at Purdue University and the colleagues with whom I interacted during my visiting semester appointment at Tulane University for all of their support.

Versions of chapters 1 and 3 were previously published in *French Literature Series* 23 (spring 1996) and *Symposium: A Quarterly Journal of Modern Foreign Languages* (spring 1997), respectively. I would like to thank the publishers of those journals, Editions Rodopi and Heldref, for the permission to reprint them.

Dr. André Langaney of the Musée de l'Homme and the staff at the Bibliothèque Nationale in Paris were steadfast in their efforts to aid my research.

And finally, much love goes now and always to my family for their enduring support. To Gilman W. Whiting I give my thanks, and my love, heart, and devotion, for being himself. And I offer all praise to the Spirits for granting me such a wonderful life.

INTRODUCTION

Theorizing Black Venus

Ve·nus [ME, fr. L. *Vener-, Venus*] 1: the Roman goddess of natural productivity and in later times of love and beauty—compare APHRODITE

The African woman belongs to the dream world of primal psychological conceptions. —Hans Werner Debrunner, *Presence to Prestige: Africans in Europe*

During the Middle Ages, between 1119 and 1142, religious scholar Peter Abelard wrote to his beloved Héloïse of the *Song of Songs:* "The bride of Canticles, an Ethiopian . . . rejoices: 'I am black but comely. . . . [and] she did well to say that because she is black and lovely therefore chosen and taken into the king's bed chamber . . . to that secret place. As far as the Ethiopian . . . such a wife prefers hidden pleasures." The erudite continues, "Besides, it so happens that the skin of black women, less agreeable to the gaze, is softer to touch and the pleasures one derives from their love are more delicious and delightful." [1] This compilation of letters, simply titled *Les Lettres complètes d'Abélard et d'Héloïse,* is studied and exalted for a variety of reasons. Yet the most memorable passages of this treasure of a text are those that matter-of-factly explain the significance of blackness and the nature of black female sexuality and black female bodies. A not-at-all odd coupling of theology and sensuality, Abelard's erotically laden explications couched in religious frames of reference mark the beginning of a sexualized narrative projected onto black women that has found its place particularly among France's nineteenth-century male literary cadre. One need not look into the obscure annals of French literary history to find a surplus of lubricious, venal black female muses.

There are of course historical and literary studies that treat French representations of and meanings ascribed to the "black," "blackness," and "Africa." Léon Fanoudh-Seifer's *Le Mythe du nègre et de l'Afrique noire dans la littérature française* critiques the overgeneralizing and stereotyping tendencies of French writers from the eighteenth century to World War II, tendencies that, for Fanoudh-Seifer, create and maintain myths of Africa and of Africans.

Léon-François Hoffman's *Le Nègre romantique: Personnage littéraire et obsession collective,* with its rich bibliography, examines the French obsession with blacks and blackness in literature from the Middle Ages to the romantic period of the nineteenth century. Christopher Miller's work, *Blank Darkness: Africanist Discourse in French,* traces the meanings of blackness and blacks in travel literature, with a particular focus on the nineteenth-century Africanist poetics of Baudelaire and Rimbaud. And finally, *White on Black: Images of Africa and Blacks in Western Popular Culture,* Jan Nederven Pieterse's seminal tricontinental endeavor, devotes several pages to the various uses of blacks in French advertising, literature, popular culture, and art.

However and more important, none of these works are feminist, and there has been to date no book-length feminist inquiry into the subject of the surplus of lubricious, venal black/mulatto female muses in the French literary and cultural imagination. Aside from explorations of Charles Baudelaire's relationship with his mulatto mistress, Jeanne Duval, captured in *Les Fleurs du mal,*[2] tangential references to Sarah Bartmann, the Hottentot Venus, and recent scholarship on Claire de Duras's *Ourika,* theoretical studies on the representations of black femininity in France is a subject that has been hitherto ignored. And those studies that seem to take up the subject function like colonizing narratives, productively putting the other to use to discuss primarily white female and/or black male sexuality. In the French cultural and literary context, this mediation of the white through the black, if you will, is especially apparent in cultural critic Sander Gilman's much cited chapter "The Hottentot and the Prostitute: Towards an Iconography of Female Sexuality," from his book *Difference and Pathology: Stereotypes of Sexuality, Race, and Madness*. Gilman's piece is frequently referred to as an example par excellence of a study of the representations of black female sexuality in France. However, one never finds any details about the one major black female figure featured in the chapter, Sarah Bartmann, the Hottentot Venus. The literal photographic presence of the black female body and her genitalia are there expressly for a better understanding of (white) patriarchy's construction/fear of female sexuality (to be read as white female sexuality). And this observation resonates in a discussion of Gilman's work in the reader *Colonial Discourse and Postcolonial Theory*. In "Introduction to Theorizing Gender," the editors refer to Gilman's text as "explor[ing] the connections between blackness and femininity, including the ways in which *white women* could be featured as approximating *black people* in their lack of evolutionary development, their 'otherness' to the norms of masculinity" (italics mine).³

The precarious position of being seen and simultaneously not seen, of invisibility, or seen invisibility as Fanon describes in his chapter "L'Expérience vécue du noir" ("The Fact of Blackness"),⁴ is one with which black women are all too familiar. That black women continue to remain at the fringes of, or better yet are excluded from, contemporary French literary criticism is to say the least interesting, given the historic French fascination with black female bodies, cemented and iconographized in the veritable person of Sarah Bartmann, given that the nineteenth century saw the birth of the major literary movements of romanticism, naturalism, and realism, whose literary productions were undeniably inflected with the French colonialist mentality of the era, and given that the "new criticism" of the late twentieth century is equally inflected with postmodernist tendencies that aim to decenter hegemony and hegemonic readings.

The turn of the century moreover saw the birth of the French film industry with the emergence of the *frères* Pathé's (1896) and Lumière's (1897) cinematic empires. While Bartmann was the in-the-flesh icon of the black female sexualized savage in the nineteenth century, American-born Josephine Baker ascended (or descended) to the spotlight in the twentieth century. Both Venuses occupied the stage, but Baker would move on to the silver screen. Her first films, *La Folie du jour*, *La Revue des Revues*, and *La Sirène des Tropiques*, were silent. With the advent of sound in the French film industry in the 1930s, Baker appeared in two talking films in the mid-1930s: *Zou Zou* and *Princesse Tam Tam*. Her third "talkie," *Fausse Alerte*, was filmed in late 1940. Situated as they were during the aftermath of the Franco-Prussian War, World War I, the French depression of 1931, and between the rumblings of World War II, the thematic trends articulated in Baker's talkies corresponded with the postwar malaise experienced in France. As an entertainer with a flair for the comic, Baker easily fit into this ever-popular genre of French film. As an outsider, a black woman from another continent, she fit neatly as well into the popular subgenre of films of the 1930s: the empire or colonial film.

According to film critic Susan Hayward, there were sixty-two empire films made in the 1930s and almost all of them refer to France's colonies in Africa.[5] The rise of *le cinéma colonial* corresponded with France's defeat in the Franco-Prussian War and a not-so-stellar performance during World War I, despite somewhat glorified stories of Verdun. France expanded its colonies to rebuild its reputation as a European power. Like travelogues and documentary films, elaborate feature films, depicting "happy savages" and exotic and lush landscapes ripe for the taking, helped to garner support for continued colonial expansion among the French spectators at home. In the colonial/empire films, France was characteristically positioned as a "civilizing force."[6] As a national and cultural apparatus, the cinema of the 1930s reflected the anxieties of the nation, but served equally as a unifying force around issues of identity and French nationalism, and as a source of escapism. Clearly aware of its weakened image as a European/Western power, gripped by "the triumvirate of fear, guilt and immobilism" at home, France via its cinema could go to its colonies (escapism) to reassure itself of its greatness as a nation (nationalism).[7] Thus, at least two of Baker's three films of this era,

Zou Zou and *Princesse Tam Tam,* take the French audience to the colonies. The latter revels in the idea of France as a paternalistic "civilizing force."

While many film critics of colonial cinema, particularly academic feminists, mention Baker's *Princesse Tam Tam,* none broach the subject as to why an African American woman specifically would be so prominently featured in this particular genre. What was it about Baker as a black woman, as an African American, that made this possible? [8] Even Hayward's important feminist and exhaustive historical work on French cinema, *French National Cinema,* does not mention the silent or talking films in which Baker costarred with the French male icons of film Jean Gabin and Albert Préjean, or Baker's *signification* in the "star system" in the context of her discussion of the "meanings" of certain representations of female sexuality on the French screen. Yet she simultaneously clearly recognizes the colonial filmic era as being important to understanding the phenomenon of French national cinema and French identity formation, and also mentions other films by Marc Allégret and Edmond Gréville, the directors of *Zou Zou* and *Princesse Tam Tam,* respectively.

Hence *Black Venus: Sexualized Savages, Primal Fears, and Primitive Narratives in French* examines French cultural, scientific, and literary representations of black femininity and the psychosexual and cultural implications of those representations. Running up against the invisibilizing tendencies of contemporary critics, this work situates black female personae at the center of its analysis of French literary history, criticism, film, and culture as figures of historical, cultural, and literary import, as keys to understanding the complexities of race, class, gender, sexuality, and racism in nineteenth-century and pre–World War II France. With the exception of the chapters devoted to the cultural and scientific icon of primitivity and sexual depravity, Sarah Bartmann, black women are both the subjects of this work and the objects of white male *literary* and *filmic* productions. The study is a unique theoretical blend of Fanonian and Morrisonian insights and feminist investigations of visuality, sexuality, and the cinema. Borrowing from feminist film discourse, I refer to the concept of the (white) male gaze as a desire to unveil, "to dissect," "to lay bare" the unknown, in this case the black female. The gaze "fixes" the black female in her place, steadies her, in order to decode and comfortably recode her into its own system of representation.[9] As Laura Mulvey writes in "Woman as Image / Man as Bearer of the Look," the (black) female caught in the male gaze will always signify male desires.[10] In his desire to illumine the dark continent of black femaleness, of racial and sexual alterity, the French male writer constructs an image that is captured in at least one particular and predominant narrative: Black Venus. Lettered men of the nineteenth and twentieth centuries were plagued by questions concerning the nature of femininity as embodied in Freud's provocative, rhetorical enunciation "*Was will das Weib?*" as well as by the more profound discovery of *other* worlds that shook the very foundation of Europe's belief in its essence, rather than incidentalness, to humanity. Desire for knowledge, and thus mastery of blacks and women, led to the creation of racist-sexist ideologies, images (sexual savages and prostitutes), and institutions (slavery and motherhood) to produce and sustain the illusion of realism, of absolute truth, thereby effecting mastery of otherness.

The specific thesis of this work then is that black women, embodying the dynamics of racial/sexual alterity, historically invoking *primal fears* and desire in European (French) men, represent ultimate difference (the *sexualized savage*) and inspire repulsion, attraction, and anxiety, which gave rise to the nineteenth-century collective French male imaginations of Black Venus (*primitive narratives*).

Theorizing the Black Venus Narrative

In her seminal study of Africanism, or "denotative and connotative blackness" in American literature, Toni Morrison writes:

As a disabling virus within literary discourses, Africanism has become, in the Eurocentric tradition . . . both a way of talking about and a way of policing matters of class, sexual license, and repression, formations and exercises of power, and meditations on ethics and accountability. . . . It provides a way of contemplating chaos and civilization, desire and fear.[11]

Africanism or the Africanist presence represents the abnormal in Eurocentric discourse; blacks, Africa, and blackness are ever-changing boundaries, pliable, makeshift moldings, always in the process of reinvention to suit Eurocentric truths. While Morrison's study of Africanism is American-specific, she recognizes that "South America, England, France, Germany, and Spain — the cultures of all these countries have participated in and contributed to some aspect of an 'invented Africa' [and its diaspora]. None has been able to persuade itself for long that criteria and knowledge could emerge outside of categories of domination." [12]

The Black Venus narrative is part of the larger discourse of Africanism in general, and French Africanism in particular. Sexual and racial differences inspire acute fears in the French male psyche. Fear is sublimated or screened through the desire to master or know this difference, resulting in the production of eroticized/exoticized narratives of truths.

Nineteenth-century literary and Baker-inspired twentieth-century filmic narratives on black femininity and accompanying images are not gratuitous. Rather, they are generally bound up with discourses of power and hierarchies. They allow certain ideas of the self and the Other to be validated. The Roman deity of beauty, Venus, was also revered as the protectress of Roman prostitutes, who in her honor erected Venus temples of worship. Within these temples, instruction in the arts of love was given to aspiring courtesans.[13] It is the latter image of prostitution, sexuality, and danger that reproduced itself in narrative and was projected onto black female bodies. The projection of the Venus image, of prostitute proclivities, onto black female bodies, allows the French writer to maintain a position of moral, sexual, and racial superiority.

Blood Strains: Exotic/Erotic Black and Mulatto Bodies
and Prostitute Proclivities

If blackness and its myriad of explications—from sun to religion—puzzled lettered men from the Middle Ages to the eighteenth century, the nineteenth century sought to naturalize racial difference and sexual proclivities, specifically black women's licentiousness, through blood discourses. Fetishized in romantic poetry and novels as well as pseudoscientific-obsessed realist and naturalist novels of the nineteenth century, black blood, *sang noir, sang-mêlé,* and *les gouttes du sang noir* have far-reaching cultural and racially sexualized implications. Black women are not only physiognomically different, but physiologically and temperamentally different. And in the case of *mulâtresses,* quadroons, and octoroons, their racialization is easily gleaned through their felinelike movements that cloak a sexually wayward predisposition.

I have afforded myself some "racial" space in my interchangeable use of the terms black female body, black women, black femininity. At times the terms refer specifically to African women, at others to mulâtresses. The idea of race, its social construction and appropriately shifting paradigms, has been greatly debated in scholarship by Henry Louis Gates Jr., Thomas Gossett, Barbara Fields, Naomi Zack, and Kwame Anthony Appiah. This racial space I accord myself certainly does not represent an attempt to erase the differences delineated by these writers. It is not a veiled attempt to replicate the very polemic—desire for sameness—that I intend to critique. Rather, the reader must keep in mind that in certain writings I note a particular black and white dichotomy, or Africanist construction, in which mulâtresses, even Creoles, are racialized into blackness. And in the case of Emile Zola's *Thérèse Raquin,* a "black" African versus "white" European juxtaposition is pervasive, despite Zola's orientalist allusion at the novel's beginning. Race, ethnicity, cultural distinctions are collapsed into one black/*nègre* stereotyped abyss. Blackness, or at least the ideas surrounding the conjoining of blackness and femininity, that is, black women, in the works of the nineteenth-century authors examined here always fall back into a discourse on domination and submission, always defer to the Black Venus master narrative.

At this juncture I feel a need to further differentiate between the imagining/writing of white femininity and black femininity. While there are certainly similarities, there are undeniable differences that are played out in a multiplicity of racially and sexually specific codes. In a comparative reading of Emile Zola's *Nana* and *Thérèse Raquin,* these differences reverberate. Both are stories of women who fall into the demimonde of Paris because of their pathological genealogies: Nana because of her lower-class origins and her family's chronic abuse of alcohol, and Thérèse, who functions as a mulâtresse, be-cause of "le sang africain de sa mère" (her mother's African blood).[14]

The contexts of Josephine Baker's scantily clad body in a banana skirt, or wild prancing to African drums in the comedy *Princesse Tam Tam,* which will be taken up in chapter 9, or singing "Haiti" enclosed in a cage in the melodramatic *Zou Zou,* and that of the muted homoeroticism of Arletty, the popular French female star of the same era, are quite different.[15] As Jacqueline Rose writes in *Sexuality and the Field of Vision,* "The cinematic image is . . . the process of representation through which sexual difference is constructed and maintained."[16] Indeed, female sexuality in general is constructed as available, deviant, and degraded. And both actresses are trans-formed into the "woman as a spectacle" for male spectators in the viewing auditorium and for the male spectators in the film. On both sides of the film they are subjected to and objectified through the male look.[17] Arletty embodies a mature, "femino-masculine eroti-cism," while Baker represents an "infantilo-innocent, but dangerous eroticism," which, according to Hayward, "satisfied voyeuristic ten-dencies without compromising the spectator. The body was eroti-cised and handed to the audience, but it was untouchable because it was [literally] imbued with [blackness and] an infantilo-innocence that kept the spectator suspended between fantasy and desire."[18] Baker's imported body, like the nineteenth-century imagined bodies, represents the colonized black female body, that is, a body trapped in an image of itself, whose primitivity, exemplified in a childlike comedic posture, sexual deviancy, degradation, and colonization, is intimately linked to racial-sexual difference.

The framework within which *Black Venus* is situated is scientific, historical, literary, filmic, and cultural, undergirded by a feminist analysis. Besides Morrison's "Africanism," which serves as the guiding theoretical basis of this study, there are, as stated earlier, Fanonisms interjected throughout. This work is informed by Fanon's acuity into the problems of "difference," "sameness," and "otherness," by a feminist hermeneutics of his critique of Manichaeanism and his radical existential phenomenology of race and racism and by his studies on dialectical materialism, and the intricacies of sexuality and culture. Indebted to Jean-Paul Sartre's analyses of overdetermination and constructivity in *Réflexions sur la question juive* (*Anti-Semite and Jew*), Fanon surmises in anguish throughout his first work, *Peau noire, masques blancs,* that the black is overdetermined from without. The black is a phobic object. And French "Negro-phobogenesis" manifests itself in the purging of drives and desires, the heaping of impurities onto a passive (fictive and incorporeal) object: "The Negro," Fanon writes, "has no ontological resistance in the eyes of the white man." [19]

In the French literary and cultural as well as filmic and scientific imaginations that are the worlds of Sarah Bartmann and Josephine Baker, black females are rendered "slaves of the idea that others have of them," slaves of their black femaleness;[20] the black female must *be* black female in relation to white males. This *being* is critical to the self-reflective/reflexive activities of overdetermination, stereotypification, and constructivity involved in the Black Venus narrative. The quintessential differences, blackness and femaleness, provide the stuff of fantastical narratives and allow French male literati, directors and their audiences, and scientists to weave them out of and into "a thousand details, anecdotes, stories." [21] Black females are perpetually ensnared, imprisoned in an essence of themselves created from without: Black Venus.

This study has been, is, and will be unsettling to some. What is more, my readings of writers of the canon as being fascinated by and paranoid about black femininity exclusive of a lengthy "foundational" exploration of the well-noted fear of (white) female sexuality will elicit incredulity from others. Nor will this work examine black masculinity. It will instead begin with the very different positionality and (mis)representation of black femininity embodied in Sarah Bartmann and carried on in fervor well into the twentieth century. Further, my choice of canonical writers, rather than "obscure" writers, is not gratuitous, but attempts to hammer home my supposition that black female bodies held a peculiarly prominent place in the French literary and cultural imagination, that their absence as subjects of contemporary criticism underscores their invisibility.

The fact that I use the word *canon* may seem particularly odd, given that the notion of the canon and the concept of canon formation has been rigorously taken to task during the last decade or so. However, French departments across the United States continue to require readings of certain authors (to the exclusion of others) as being representative of certain literary movements and their respective centuries—often before graduate students embark upon various areas of specialization. In effect, the canon exists and the authors constituting such a French canon undeniably *played in feminized darkness*.

I could have had this study begin with as early a period as the Middle Ages, that is, with Peter Abelard's *Lettres*, continued into the classical period with Paul Scarron's *Epistre chagrin* and La Fontaine's black-white woman Psiché, and mulled through scores of asides, footnote references, and quasi-scientific studies on black women in the Age of Enlightenment, by the likes of Denis Diderot, Buffon, and others. However, the amount of material would have been vast, and there are studies, although certainly not enough of them, that chronicle images of blacks in France. The nineteenth century witnessed the most extensive contact with blacks from the French slave trade and colonial system in the Antilles to the colonization of sub-Saharan Africa in the late nineteenth century. In addition, nineteenth-century France was allowed a privileged look at Sarah

Bartmann, whose influence on the French male psyche spanned high and low culture. But more important, the nineteenth century is the only century in which at least six writers — Balzac, de Pons, Baudelaire, Zola, Maupassant, and Loti [22] — rhapsodized and obsessed over racialized heroines.

The texts by the authors covered in this study, invoking the themes and intersections of race, sexuality, racism, and gender, are in fact representative works of the various nineteenth-century literary schools of thought as well as of the authors themselves. That is, aside from Charles Baudelaire's Jeanne Duval cycle of poems in *Les Fleurs du mal,* these novellas, as well as Baudelaire's prose poem *La Belle Dorothée,* [23] are the only existing pieces of literature by these authors that employ the Black Venus narrative, that conflate the black female body with the sexualized savage, that have racialized female protagonists as objects of desire and abjection.

The inclusion of film in this primarily literary study is an attempt to demonstrate a continuum of the Black Venus narrative in the modern French cultural imagination that transcends mediums and the ways in which Josephine Baker's screen image, her venal em*bodi*ment, was put to use to maintain French interests. The Black Venus narrative, in this instance, works hand in glove with the goals of *le cinéma colonial.*

This study begins by exploring, in chapter 1, "Writing Sex, Writing Difference: Creating the Master Text on the Hottentot Venus," the tragic life and career of Sarah Bartmann, the Hottentot Venus, as the personification of French male imaginations of black women. It also presents the scarcely known vaudeville *La Vénus hottentote, ou haine aux Françaises,* translated in the appendix of this work and discussed in chapter 2, "Representing Sarah — Same Difference or No Difference at All? *La Vénus hottentote, ou haine aux Françaises.*" The vaudeville appropriates Bartmann's persona and simultaneously reduces her to an object of derision.

In covering the literary movements of nineteenth-century France, this work moves thematically rather than chronologically. Hence, at the conclusion of chapter 2 I take up a reading of romantic realist Honoré de Balzac's *La Fille aux yeux d'or* as I allude to the similarities between the desire to purge racial difference in the denouements of *La Vénus hottentote* and those of *La Fille aux yeux d'or.* In chapter 3, " 'The Other Woman': Reading a Body of Difference in Balzac's *La Fille aux yeux d'or*," I eschew the traditional orientalist readings of Balzac's sex slave qua heroine Paquita Valdès for a biracialized reading of her exotic origins, reified in her Antillean place of birth.

Romantic poet Gaspard de Pons's *Ourika, l'Africaine* — the focus of chapter 4, "Black Blood, White Masks, and Négresse Sexuality in de Pons's *Ourika, l'Africaine*" — is a reworking in form and content of Mme. Claire de Duras's celebrated tale *Ourika*. The story of a young Senegalese woman imported to France as a "pet" of sorts to an aristocratic family, Ourika discovers she is afflicted with blackness and will therefore never marry. De Pons's poem transforms the pious, self-loathing Ourika into a raging, sexualized stereotype. She becomes the counterpart to Othello, whose civil exterior is only a front for a smoldering African interior.

Renowned for his avid encounters with otherness and adoration of variously hued bodies, the poet Charles Baudelaire wrote *La Belle Dorothée* as part autobiography, part fiction.[24] Dorothée is a prostitute from one of the French colonies. But more important, the veritable muse for Dorothée was not Jeanne Duval, the poet's longtime mulatto mistress, but an etching of a Khoikhoi woman from a historiographical text, as I point out in chapter 5, "Black Is the Difference: Identity, Colonialism, and Fetishism in *La Belle Dorothée*." Within this prose poem is the specter of Sarah Bartmann and the conflation of the Black Venus narrative and the "Hottentot" as prostitute.

In chapter 6, "Desirous and Dangerous Imaginations: The Black Female Body and the Courtesan in Zola's *Thérèse Raquin*," I demonstrate that the conflation of the black body and prostitute proclivities weighs heavily in naturalist Emile Zola's *Thérèse Raquin*. Using Alexandre Parent-Duchâtelet's groundbreaking study on nineteenth-century prostitution in Paris, *La Prostitution à Paris au XIXème siècle*, as well as Sander Gilman's rather contentious study of the conflation of the black female body and prostitute body in *Difference and Pathology: Stereotypes of Sexuality, Race, and Madness*, I take up in this chapter the fascination with mulatto bodies in the nineteenth century and the wayward sexuality attributable to their racialization.

Parent-Duchâtelet's study provides the kernels of what one could certainly refer to as "the science of prostitution" in nineteenth-century France. His work would not only inform other studies on prostitutes and dictate public policy on regulation and health-related issues involving prostitution, but would also inform scores of fictional works in their portraitures of the prostitute and her proclivities. While Sander Gilman's *Difference and Pathology* assists in depicting the cultural factors that led to the conflation of the prostitute body with the black body, Parent-Duchâtelet's *La Prostitution* presents critical demographic data on prostitutes that help to clarify/demystify the numbers of black women potentially involved in the sex trade in the Paris of Zola's day.

In chapter 7, "Can a White Man Love a Black Woman? Perversions of Love beyond the Pale in Maupassant's 'Boitelle,' " I explore another literary work that can be characterized as realist with naturalist tendencies. However, Guy de Maupassant's "Boitelle" stands apart as a text that sympathetically broaches the subject of racial prejudice through an interracial love plot. Yet the "love" is tempered with exoticism and presents us with this question "Can a White Man Love a Black Woman?," which is diametrically opposed to the question concerning authentic love, inferiority, and black disalienation posed by Frantz Fanon in *Black Skin, White Masks.*

Chapter 8, "Bamboulas, Bacchanals, and Dark Veils over White Memories in Loti's *Le Roman d'un spahi,*" examines Pierre Loti's highly inflammatory yet sentimental novel. Although *Le Roman* is read by contemporary critics as a continuation of Loti's orientalist fascination, this chapter argues that it is an Africanist work. Replete with stereotypes of blackness and black women, Loti's work, unlike that of Maupassant, outlines the perils (to white men) of interracial sex.

While this book begins with discussions of Sarah Bartmann, chapter 9, "Cinematic Venus in the Africanist Orient," concludes with an analysis of the popular films of Josephine Baker. The Baker biography, including her war heroism, "Rainbow tribe," and personal agency, is not of particular interest here. Rather, it is the Baker screen image that is germane. With its orientalist and Africanist themes, her colonial comedy film, *Princesse Tam Tam*, is read as a filmic representation of the Black Venus narrative. In effect, Baker performs Black Venus.

It is only fitting that a feminist work on black women as sexual objects should conclude with thoughts and writings by black women. The epilogue wrestles with questions of subversion, agency, and resistance. Black feminist thoughts and practices are at the helm of this section, which closes with an important discussion of the work of nineteenth- and twentieth-century Francophone Caribbean women writers of color, such as Marie Chauvet's and Myriam Warner-Vieyra's oppositional re-presentations of black women as subjects of history.

1

Writing Sex, Writing Difference:

Creating the Master Text on the Hottentot Venus

Cuvier

Science, science, science!
Everything is beautiful

Cranial measurements
crowd my notebook pages,

and I am moving closer,
close to how these numbers

signify aspects of
national character

Her genitalia
will float inside a labeled

pickling jar in the Musée
de l'Homme on a shelf

above Broca's brain:
"The Venus Hottentot."

The preceding excerpt from Elizabeth Alexander's poetic master-piece *The Venus Hottentot* tersely recounts a definitive moment in the history of sexual science as it intersects with race, a moment

DUKE

UNIVERSITY

PRESS · PUBLICITY

BOX 90660

DURHAM, NC

27708-0660

Michael Taeckens
PUBLICITY

(919) 687-3639
TELEPHONE

(919) 688-4391
FAX

taeckens@acpub.duke.edu
EMAIL

REVIEW COPY

BLACK VENUS

Sexualized Savages, Primal Fears, and Primitive Narratives in French

T. Denean Sharpley-Whiting

Price:

(0-8223-2340-0) $17.95
(0-8223-2307-9) $49.95

(Please note that unjacketed cloth editions are primarily for library use. Non-library reviewers should quote the paperback price.)

Publication Date: July 1, 1999

*Please send two copies of the published review.

when science and ideology merged and a black woman's body mediated the tenuous relationship between the two—a moment when celebrated French anatomist and naturalist Georges Cuvier met the equally celebrated cadaver of Sarah Bartmann, the Hottentot Venus, a South African woman exhibited throughout England and France for some five years because of her "remarkable formation of person."

Notwithstanding Sander Gilman's seminal work *Difference and Pathology*,[1] little is known about either Bartmann's exhibition or about the public and popular responses to her exhibitions in France. And even less is known about Sarah Bartmann the person; mystery surrounds her date of birth, her date of death, her racial/ethnic origins—was she a Hottentot (Khoikhoi), a female Bushman (San), or a *sang-mêlé?* One can only speculate and approximate. But given the circumstances under which she was thrust into the limelight in the nineteenth century, these voids are not unusual. Most nineteenth-century French spectators did not view her as a person or even a human, but rather as a titillating curiosity, a collage of buttocks and genitalia.

For the scientific community she provided the missing link in "the great chain of being," the crucial step between humanity, that is, Europeans, and animals.[2] Indeed, among all the explorative undertakings of the French nineteenth-century medical community, this African woman figures as a treasured find, the key to the origin of an inferior species. As Georges Cuvier indicates, her body served in an equal degree as the master text on black female sexuality for Europe's scientific community.[3] It is the intention of this chapter not only to read excerpts from this phantasmal master text, but, more important, to relate Bartmann's immense influence on nineteenth-century Western racial-sexual science.

Born in Kaffraria in the interior of the Cape Colony of South Africa in approximately 1788, and renamed Saartjie Baartman when the region came under Dutch colonial rule, Baartman was one of six siblings. Her father was a drover of cattle who was killed by neighboring San, and her mother died when she was two years old. Her husband was a drummer, and she had had one child, who died shortly after birth.[4] She became a domestic of sorts to a Boer farmer, Peter Cezar, at the Cape of Good Hope.[5]

At the age of twenty-one or twenty-two, on October 29, 1810, Saartjie entered into a contractual agreement with Alexander Dunlop of St. James, Middlesex, England, a surgeon of an African ship, and Hendrik Cezar, the brother of Peter Cezar. The contract stipulated that in addition to performing domestic duties, she was to be exhibited in England and Ireland. She would be paid a portion of the profits from her exhibition and repatriated in five years. However, upon Baartman's arrival in London, Dunlop attempted to sell his share in the "Hottentot," as well as the skin of a giraffe, to William Bullock, director of the Liverpool Museum in London. In offering the Baartman, Dunlop described her as having "a very singular appearance" and predicted that "she would make a fortune for anyone who shewed [*sic*] her in London."[6] Bullock passed on both propositions.

In September 1810, Baartman was exhibited at 225 Piccadilly. The advertising bill read: "Parties of Twelve and upwards, may be accommodated with Private Exhibition of the Hottentot, at No. 225 Piccadilly, between Seven and Eight O'clock in the Evening, by giving notice to the Door-keeper the Day previous."[7]

Standing a mere four feet six inches tall, Baartman's miniature frame was weighed down by her abundant buttocks. It was this riveting attribute, "large as a cauldron pot," as one bawdy English ballad attests,[8] that Europeans paid to see.

A sensation in England, leaving in her wake street ballads, caricatures, an appearance in the Chancery Court of England, and a name change to Sarah Bartmann[9] in December 1811, literally carrying her fortune behind her, Bartmann and her protuberant charms found themselves again in the limelight upon her arrival in Paris in September 1814. She and Cezar parted company in Paris; her new guardian was a showman of wild animals named Réaux. According to the widely read *Journal des dames et des modes:* "The doors of the salon open, and the Hottentot Venus could be seen entering. She is a 'Callipygian Venus.' Candies are given to her in order to entice her

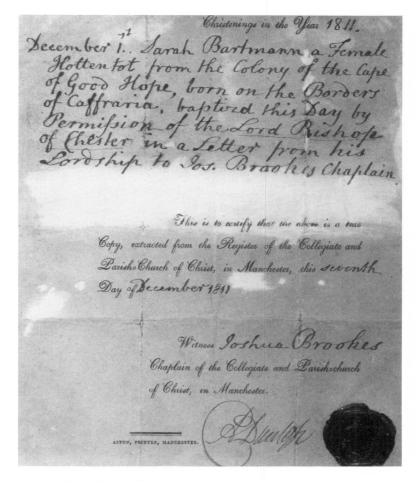

Baptismal certificate of Sarah Bartmann (December 7, 1811). Courtesy of the Musée de l'Homme, Paris.

to leap about and sing; she is told that she is the prettiest woman in all society." [10]

The price to view this one-woman spectacle was three francs. At rue de Castiglione and for the same admission price, Réaux was also exhibiting a five-year-old male rhinoceros. Bartmann was exhibited from 11 A.M. to 10 P.M. at the ground level of 188, rue Saint-Honoré.

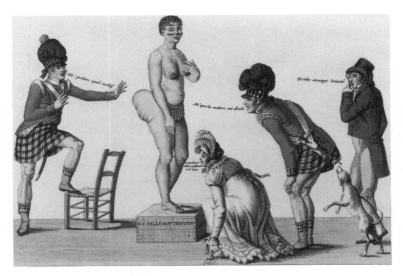

Les Curieux en extase ou les cordons de souliers (1814). Courtesy of the Bibliothèque Nationale, Paris.

La Vénus hottentote (1814). Courtesy of the Bibliothèque Nationale, Paris.

Just as in England, Bartmann's persona filtered into satirical cartoons such as the ones titled Les Curieux en extase ou les cordons de souliers ("The curious in ecstasy or shoelaces") and La Vénus hottentote. In Les Curieux en extase, in which the French cartoonist pokes fun at the British fascination with the Venus, Bartmann is displayed on a pedestal engraved with LA BELLE HOTTENTOTE. She has arrested the gaze of three men, two British soldiers and one male civilian, and a female civilian. There is also a dog in the drawing, representing the base, animal-like nature of the human spectators, the proverbial "we are all animals" sentiment, and participating in its own sort of voyeurism as it looks under the kilt of one of the Englishmen. Each character comments on Bartmann's body. One soldier, behind Bartmann, extends his hand as if to touch her buttocks and proclaims, "Oh, godem, quel rosbif!" (Oh, goddamn, what roast beef!). The other soldier, looking directly into her genitalia, remarks: "Ah, que la nature est drôle!" (Ah, how amusing nature is!). The male civilian, peering through lorgnettes, declares: "Qu'elle étrange beauté!" (What strange beauty!), while the female civilian, bending down to tie her shoelaces—hence the cartoon's subtitle—looks through Bartmann's legs and utters: "A quelque chose malheureux est bon" (From some points of view misfortune can be good). The woman is, however, looking not at the "Hottentot," but through the opening between her legs and up the kilt of the soldier behind Bartmann. Thus, from her angle, she sees through Bartmann's "misfortune," her openness, or rather, the opening between her legs, something more pleasing. Bartmann's body is inscribed upon from the various perspectives. She becomes, all at once, roast beef, a strange beauty, an amusing freak of nature, and erased, invisible, as the female spectator privileges the penis. And while the points of view appear to reflect different positionalities, the ways of seeing the Other as exotic, amusing, invisible, and as something to be eaten or consumed like roast beef reflect sameness.

Bartmann was not only the subject of cartoons, but also of a popular vaudeville show at the Théâtre de Vaudeville entitled *La Vénus hottentote, ou haine aux Françaises.* A one-act vaudeville written by

Théaulon, Dartois, and Brasier, the piece was first performed on November 19, 1814.[11] On and off stage, from cartoons to theater, Bartmann's body inspired a collective French obsession. And at the height of her career, the most profound evidence of her impact on the French imagination manifested itself among the medical community in the person of France's renowned naturalist Georges Cuvier.

For three days in March 1815 at the Jardin du Roi, at the request of Cuvier and with the permission of her guardian Réaux, a team of zoologists, anatomists, and physiologists examined Bartmann. The subsequent findings from this examination were published in 1824 in Frédéric Cuvier's and Geoffroy St.-Hilaire's *Histoire naturelle des mammifères* and later in 1864 in *Discours sur les révolutions du globe* by Georges Cuvier et al. The prefatory note of *Histoire naturelle* explains the necessity for the text and its goals:

> The work that we have published has been requested and deemed necessary for many years by naturalists. . . . *The Natural History of Mammals* consequently proposes two problems: (1) the relationship that exists between these animals, and (2) the role that they play within the general economy of nature, that is, their relationship with other beings.[12]

The discipline of natural history is a combination of scientific writing, history, and ethnography that allows objects under the gaze to be ordered into a totalizing system of representation, that allows the seen body to become the known body. A significant problem within the constitutive framework of the discipline arises because of its dependency on the human eye. The human eye is faulty, often creating illusory images because of its "blind spot." Martin Jay notes in *Downcast Eyes: The Denigration of Vision in Twentieth-Century French Thought* that "the human eye has a blind spot where the optic nerve connects with the retina. . . . The blind spot's existence suggests a metaphoric 'hole' in vision."[13] Within this hole or empty space, alterity is invested.

Bartmann will be placed within this hole in the European system of representation as a highly developed animal, and then closely scrutinized in order to determine her relationship to other animals and human beings. She will be used as a yardstick by which to judge the stages of Western evolution, by which to discern identity, difference, and progress.

During the three-day examination, Cuvier asked Bartmann if she would allow herself to be painted nude. In that same prefatory note, the authors offer an explanation for the inclusion of etchings in the volume:

Our drawings present each animal in a simple state and always in a profile because it is in this position that one can best seize the totality of the form and physiognomy; and we have taken care to provide a frontal drawing where necessary in order to better see and judge the animals.

The profile drawings permit the viewer to "best seize the totality of the form and physiognomy," "to better see and judge the animals." Seizing, seeing, judging, provided by the tool of the cameralike eye, are essential to the naturalist's project. The sketches, yielding up Bartmann's body, provide more visual clarity so that the gaze can fixate on the body in order to contemplate its anomalies. The sketches allow the viewer to observe, document, and compare her various physiognomic and physiological differences, differences that vastly differentiate the Other from the European self. Through this comparative/definitive exercise, Bartmann will be relegated to the terrain of the primitive—the lowest exemplum of the human species—while the European will always assume the pinnacle of human development. This process of mediating the self, of reflecting the self, through the body of the black female Other begins and rebegins with every regard.

Of his initial observations, Georges Cuvier writes in *Discours sur les révolutions du globe:*

When we met her for the first time, she believed herself to be about 26 years old. . . . Everyone who had been able to see her over the course of eighteen months in our capital could verify the enormous protuberance of her buttocks and the brutal appearance of her face. . . . Her movements had something of a brusqueness and unexpectedness, reminiscent of those of a monkey. In particular, she had a way of pushing out her lips in the same manner we have observed in the Orangutan. Her personality was happy, her memory good, after several weeks she recognized a person that she had only seen one time. . . . she spoke tolerably good Dutch, which she learned at the Cape. . . . also knew a little English . . . was beginning to say a few words of French; she danced in the fashion of her country and played with a fairly good ear upon a little instrument she called a Jew's Harp. Necklaces, belts, pieces of colored glass, and other savage trumperies seemed very much to please her; but that which flattered her taste above all else was brandy. (214) [14]

Cuvier's description abounds with associations of black femaleness with bestiality and primitivism. Further, by way of contemplating Bartmann as a learned, domesticated beast — comparing her to an orangutan — he reduces her facility with languages, her good memory, and musical inclinations to a sort of simianlike mimicry of the European race. By the nineteenth century, the ape, the monkey, and orangutan had become the interchangeable counterparts, the next of kin, to blacks in pseudoscientific and literary texts.[15]

Under the ever so watchful eyes and the pen of the naturalist, the master text on the black female body is created; the light of white maleness illumines this dark continent:

Her conformation was initially striking because of the enormous width of her hips, which surpassed forty-two inches, and because of the protrusion of her buttocks, which were more than half a foot. Of the remaining body parts, she had no other deformities: her shoulders, her back, the top of her chest were graceful. The bulging out of her stomach was not at all excessive. Her arms, a bit thin, were very well made, and her hand was charming. Her foot was also very alluring. (214)

Cuvier's gaze, it appears, is tempered with eroticism. The hand, foot, and other body parts, endowed with grace, charm, and allure, become a synecdoche for the palpably titillating black female body. As he views Sarah Bartmann displayed before him nude, the scientist is as captivated by the Venus's charms as the male spectators at her rue St. Honoré exhibitions. Even Bartmann's belly bulge was not, for the equally short and paunchy Cuvier, disproportionate; rather, it was congruous with her beguiling arms, hands, and other extremities.

Wrenched from the seductive reverie induced by this African Delilah, the scientist violently readjusts his optic receiver and pen. Mistakenly identifying Bartmann as a San (Bushman), "people more backward than the Hottentots," instead of as a Khoikhoi (211), the now libidinally divested Cuvier observes:

That which our female Bushman possessed that was the most repulsive was her physiognomy. Her face takes in part after the Negro by the jutting out of the jaw, the obliquity of the incisor teeth, the thickness of lips, the shortness . . . of chin . . . and in part after the Mongol by the enormity of the cheek bones, the flatness of the base of the nose. . . . Her hair was black and woolly like that of Negroes, the slits of her eyes were horizontal . . . like that of Mongols . . . her eyes were dark and lively; her lips, a bit blackish, and monstrously swelled; her complexion very swarthy. . . . Her ears were much like those found in many monkeys, small and weakly formed at the tragus. (214–15)

Cuvier reads Bartmann's face according to perceived racially specific characteristics. In this classificatory discourse based upon the all-knowing scientific gaze, he determines that Bartmann is a racial admixture: in part Negro because of her protruding jaw, short chin, pointy, cannibal-like incisor teeth, and woolly hair, and in part Mongol because of the slant of her eyes and large cheekbones. Her appearance insults his culturally biased aesthetic sensibilities. As he gazes back toward classical antiquity for icons of idyllic beauty and form,[16] Bartmann's starkly different — "swarthy" — complexion, monstrously swollen blackish lips, and anatomical and other physiognomic characteristics strike him as being so far removed from his ideals of beauty and goodness that he is moved again to find some relationship between her ears and those of a monkey. In negotiating Bartmann's tenuous place in the "great chain of being," he defini-

tively concludes that the aforementioned characteristics are reminiscent of monkeys ("des singes") and forever destines blacks to a
state of barbarity ("toujours restées barbares").[17]

In addition to the protuberant buttocks, which were not at all,
according to the scientist, "muscular, but a mass of a shaking and
elastic consistency, vibrating with the woman's every move" (215)
and her "rebutante physionomie" (214), Cuvier describes at length
Bartmann's massive hanging breasts:

Her breasts, usually lifted and held in place by her clothing, when left
alone were a large hanging mass which terminated obliquely in a blackish aureole of more than four inches in diameter pitted with radiating
wrinkles, near the center of which was a nipple so flattened and oblit-
erated that it was barely visible: the general color of her skin was a
yellowish-brown, almost as dark as her face; and she had no body hair
apart from a few short flecks of wool, similar to that on her head, scattered about her organs of regeneration. (214–15)

Breasts, the visible symbol of feminine seductive charm and of suck-
ling, attracted particular interest in the medical literature of the eighteenth and nineteenth centuries.[18] According to eighteenth-century
sexologist L. C. H. Macquart, "Nature destined the organ to nurture
the new-born human being; she gave the breast a seductive charm
by virtue of its form and bloom which powerfully attract men."[19]
Bartmann's breasts, like her buttocks, represent for Cuvier an overdevelopment of female sexuality, a gross exaggeration of normalcy.
She is excess (218).

However, at this juncture Cuvier's text on black female sexuality
and blackness remains superficial and incomplete. Or better yet, the
text merely replicates earlier ethnographic works on Africans that
had such words as *savage, primitive, monkey,* and *hideous* liberally
sprinkled throughout them. As an anatomist, who at this moment of
interpreting a black female body was wading in the waters of theo-
ries in keeping with polygenesis, Cuvier endeavored to prove that
blacks were not only physiognomically and physiologically distinct,
but that black women were anatomically different. And what be-

comes crucial to his project lies in her organ of reproduction. Even in Bartmann's nakedness, Cuvier had yet to decipher her body, to undress the body. In the nineteenth century it is only through dissection that the hidden secrets of the body are fully revealed to the medical gaze,[20] and Bartmann still wore the veil of her skin.

The opportunity for dissection later presented itself, for on December 29, 1815, or January 1, 1816,[21] when she was mistakenly treated for a catarrh, a pleurisy, and dropsy of the breast, Sarah Bartmann died of smallpox aggravated by alcohol poisoning. Immediately following her death, Cuvier obtained permission from the prefect of police to examine Bartmann's body in greater detail. Again taking her to the Jardin du Roi, he began his groundbreaking anatomical study.

Cuvier made a plaster molding of her body. Realizing the importance of his study to the science of natural history, he immediately unveiled Bartmann. The protuberant charms of the Venus were still a curiosity. He discovered that underneath the buttocks, there was nothing but "une masse de graisse" (a mass of fat) (218). Attempting to solve concretely the riddle of the buttocks with respect to the cause of the excessive development, Cuvier writes that on the occasion of her first visit to the Jardin du Roi Bartmann "assured us that this undeniably bizarre conformation occurs during the first pregnancy." (218)

Bartmann's "monstrous" steatopygia was quickly superseded by the treasure Cuvier discovered between her thighs (218): "We did not at all perceive the more remarkable particularity of her organization; she held her apron ('tablier') carefully hidden, it was between her thighs, and it was not until after her death that we knew she had it" (215–16). The famous "Hottentot apron" is a hypertrophy, or overdevelopment, of the labia minora, or nymphae. The apron was one of the most widely discussed riddles of female sexuality in the nineteenth century. However, its existence, its intriguing origins, and its uses had been greatly debated in various travelogues of the eighteenth century. As Cuvier began his tract on the Venus, he noted: "There is nothing more famous in natural history than the apron of the Hottentots, and at the same time nothing has been the object of so many debates" (211). Some historiographers of the eighteenth century, such as French naturalist François Le Vaillant, thought that the apron — which he regarded as a monstrous example of a few African women's attempts at coquetry and fashion — was the prolongation of the outer vaginal lips, while others, like Englishman John Barrow, surmised that it was a natural development of the nymphae or "petites lèvres." [22] The writings of Le Vaillant and Barrow informed the work of their successor Cuvier, who while not the first naturalist to interest himself in the bodies of black women, was the first to dissect a black female cadaver of Bartmann's stature and to solve definitively at least one part of the apron's mysterious puzzle.

Performing a very thorough examination of Bartmann's genitalia, Cuvier notes:

The apron . . . is a development of the nymphae. . . . The outer lips, scarcely pronounced, were intercepted by an oval of four inches; from the upper angle descended between them a quasi-cylindrical protuberance of around eighteen lines long and over six lines thick, whose lower extremity enlarges, splits, and protrudes like two fleshy, rippled petals of two and a half inches in length and roughly one inch in width. Each one is rounded at the tip; their base enlarges and descends along the internal border of the outer lip of its side and changes into a fleshy crest. . . . If one assembles these two appendages, together they form a heart-shaped figure . . . in which the middle would be occupied by the vulva. . . . As for the idea that these excrescences are a product of art, it appears well refuted today if it is true that all Bushwomen possess them from youth. The one that we have seen probably did not take pleasure in procuring such an ornament of which she was ashamed, thus hid so carefully. (216–18)

This very detailed examination of Bartmann's sex, proceeding by the nominating of the visible, consists of Cuvier's use of measurements, adjectives, and metaphors. His language is flowery and feminine: fleshy, rippled petals, crests, and heart-shaped figures. Bartmann's sex blooms, blossoms, before his very eyes; the body becomes legible. As he reads and simultaneously writes a text on Bartmann, the mystery of the dark continent unfolds. The *tablier* is nothing more than the overdevelopment of the nymphae caused by the hot climates in Africa: "We know that the development of the nymphae varies much in Europe, yet it becomes in general more considerable in hotter countries" (217). Moreover, because Bartmann refused to show Cuvier the tablier, which for Khoikhoi women was culturally a demonstration of disrespect, and because the tablier does not conform to European cultural standards of beauty and art, Cuvier racially naturalizes—in a few short paragraphs—its existence, suggesting primitivity, and consequently a difference in comparison to European women's sex.

Unlike his predecessor Le Vaillant and his undeniably Eurocentric ideals concerning the tablier, Cuvier is not interested in the apron's possible cultural significations; it is not a product of art because it is not beautiful; it is not even a "monstrous" signifier of coquetry because it is not alluring to his gaze; and it is certainly not fashionable because it is not *à la mode française*. The tablier had to be deemed a racially specific characteristic,[23] and thus representative of sexual pathology, in order to shore up claims of Africans' primitive origins.[24]

Nonetheless, for Cuvier, the tablier itself does not establish "a rapport between the women and monkeys," since monkeys' nymphae are barely visible (218). It is "ces énormes masses de graisse que les Boschimanes portent sur les fesses [qui] . . . offrent une ressemblance frappante aux femelles des mandrills" (these enormous masses of fat that the Bushwomen carry on the buttocks which . . . offer a striking resemblance to female mandrills) (218). Because of this "accroissement vraiment monstreux" (veritable monstrous growth) (218), Cuvier searches for a skeletal modification. Hence, the deciphering and dissecting does not stop at her genitalia. Examining the interior of her vulva and womb, and finding nothing particularly different, he moves on to her "compressed" and "depressed" skull and her pelvic bone ("les os du bassin"). Comparing her pelvic bone against "négresses" and "différentes femmes blanches," he concludes that Negro women share characteristics with female Bushmen and that these characteristics are similar to those of female monkeys ("des femelles singes") (218):

> I was curious to know if the pelvic bones had experienced some modification from this extraordinary overload that they carry. I have thus compared the pelvis of my Bushman female with those of negresses and of different white women; I have found it to be more similar to the first, that is to say, proportionally smaller, less flared. . . . All these characteristics link, but with a quantity nearly imperceptible, the negresses and the Bushmen females with female monkeys. (218–19)

Courtesy of the scientist's trained anatomical eye, Bartmann's body attests not only to black women's nearly imperceptible evolutionary underdevelopment, but through Cuvier's use of phrenology — a pseudoscientific discourse that maintains that character and intellect can be read through the shape of the skull and "voluminousness" of the brain — wholly affirms black inferiority (221). Neither the Bushmen "ni aucune race de nègres" (nor any race of Negroes) (221), according to Cuvier, could have been remotely responsible for the birth of Egyptian civilization (221). The naturalist "could easily assure" his reader that "they [Egyptians] belonged to the same race of men as us; that they had very voluminous skulls and brains; that in a word they were not the exception to that cruel law which seems to have condemned to an eternal inferiority races with depressed and compressed skulls" (221–22). Stressing difference physiologically ("une ressemblance frappante avec celles qui surviennent aux femelles des mandrills, des papious, etc."), physiognomically ("rebutante physiognomie"), and phrenologically ("crane déprimé and comprimé"), this nineteenth-century master text on the black female body reads as ultimate *difference* and *pathology*.

Besides molding Bartmann's entire body in plaster, Cuvier preserved her genitalia and skeleton. And in 1816, closing his chapter on the black female body, he "had the honor of presenting the genital organs of this woman to the Académie, prepared in a manner so as not to leave any doubt about the nature of her apron" (216). Cuvier's work greatly influenced other nineteenth-century anatomical studies on black women throughout Europe, the Antilles, and the United States.

Today Sarah Bartmann's remains are safely tucked away in Paris's Musée de l'Homme. According to the museum's director, André Langaney, the plaster body molding of Bartmann caused such excitement among museum visitors (one of the female tour guides was allegedly sexually accosted, and the molding itself had become the object of touching and many amorous masturbatory liaisons) that its exhibition was discontinued. It appears that Sarah Bartmann, sadly and ironically commemorated in song, theater, and plaster, alive or dead remained a curious spectacle capable of inciting sexual frenzy and fervor well into the latter half of the twentieth century.

2

Representing Sarah — Same Difference or No Difference at All? *La Vénus hottentote, ou haine aux Françaises*

Sometime during the early quarter of the twentieth century, the esteemed director of Paris's Musée de l'Homme, Professor Verneau, wrote in ire of the continued popularity of the long-dead Hottentot Venus, Sarah Bartmann. "[It is her] enormous steatopygia," declared the director, "that excites many of the visitors to our collections."[1] Bartmann, who, as we have seen, was brought to Paris in September 1814 for purposes of exhibiting her buttocks, found herself, or at least parts of herself, at the center of Parisian popular culture.

But perhaps the most astounding example of Sarah Bartmann's popularity in the French cultural imagination was the production of a vaudeville entitled *La Vénus hottentote, ou haine aux Françaises.*[2] A "one-act vaudeville," *The Hottentot Venus* was written in 1814 by Messieurs Théaulon, Dartois, and Brasier.

The comedy made its debut on November 19, 1814, at the Théâtre de Vaudeville, just two months after Bartmann's arrival in Paris. The Théâtre de Vaudeville's musical director, Doche, composed and arranged thirty-four airs, including a "Hottentot" song for the musical comedy. The vaudeville used the same performers for its entire run of thirteen months: Messieurs Isambert, Hipolite, Séveste, Mesdemoiselles Rivière, Bodin, Betzi, and Madame Lenoble. Bartmann died on December 29, 1815. However, the last performance, triple-billed with *Les Visites* and *Madame Favart,* was given on January 4, 1815.

Although Bartmann's exhibition at 188, rue St. Honoré, just blocks away from the théâtre, coincided with the vaudeville's run, she was not in the piece. She was caricatured by a white female actress, Mademoiselle Rivière. And it is only at the vaudeville's end that a portrait of Bartmann's "beauté effrayante" (frightening beauty) is conspicuously presented (11).

Vaudeville represents an interactive genre of jocular performativity that combines dialogue, dance, song, and pantomime. Vaudeville provides a hermeneutics of culture, since its effectiveness depends wholly on audience participation.[3] The interactive comedic or joking aspect of this cultural production allows for insight into the significance of the performance as a segue into the political unconscious of the culture.

Jokes are explicitly linked to the production of pleasure. But jokes equally, according to Freud, carry implicit and insidious judgments about the object or objects of the joke:

Joking . . . is an activity which aims at deriving pleasure from mental processes. . . . Where a joke is not an aim in itself—that is, where it is not an innocent one—there are only two purposes that it may serve, and these two can themselves be subsumed under a single heading. It is either a hostile joke (serving the purpose of aggressiveness, satire, or defence) or an obscene joke (serving the purpose of exposure).[4]

The jocular nature of this performance places it in the hostile aggressiveness category that allows one "to exploit something ridiculous in another," in this case, Bartmann's *beauté effrayante,* savagery, and her buttocks. The vaudeville will further "bribe the third party (the audience) with its yield of pleasure into taking sides with the interlocutors (the actors/writers) of the joke without very close investigation."[5]

Replete with dangerous liaisons, both incestuous and interracial, *The Hottentot Venus* plays upon the idea of difference and sameness within categories of racial/ethnic stereotypes. As Hal Foster notes in *Recodings: Art, Spectacle, Cultural Politics:*

The other is structurally necessary, for it defines the limits of bourgeois social text—what is (a)social, (ab)normal, (sub)cultural. In short, order is produced around the positioning of the other by which (on the social level) it is made marginal and (on the historical level) suspended as exotic or "primitive." Exclusionary stereotypes, which effectively turn the other into a "pure object, a spectacle, a clown" (Barthes), have long comprised a principal mode of this control.[6]

Indeed, I would argue that although exemplifying Parisian's Bartmannmania, the vaudeville implicates itself more as a narcissistic venture, a call "to order," however cloaked in comedic verbiage, for a reaffirmation of Frenchwomen as erotic objects of the white male gaze,[7] and conversely for Bartmann's reduction to the "enormous butt" of a joke. To reduce Sarah Bartmann to an object of derision, "a spectacle, a clown," is to strip away her sexual appeal, albeit perverse and objectified, to the French male spectator, to reinforce and reinscribe Bartmann's position in the Manichaean social world as a primitive savage.

The gaze is always bound up with power, domination, and eroticization; it is eroticizing, sexualized, and sexualizing. The indisputable fact that throngs of a predominantly male, French crowd paid to gaze upon Bartmann as the essential primitive, as the undeveloped savage unable to measure up to Frenchness, is undercut by her practically au naturel presentation. From a purely ethnographic standpoint, her unveiling, the essentially nude exhibition, except for the apron that covered her genitalia, allows one to "best seize" her remarkable formation. There is of course, as Laura Mulvey writes, pleasure in this looking; there is repressed desire in it. For as much as the *apron* covers Bartmann, it also thwarts the unveiling, the ocular seizing needed to judge, to see all and beyond, bound up with the act of looking. The male spectator will return time and time again to imagine what is behind the "veil" (apron), so to speak, to discern the sexual mysteries of Africa.

Yet the comedy's intentions of redirecting the gaze have still more far-reaching and insidious cultural implications. The de-eroticization of the French male gaze with respect to black women (embodied in the objectified Sarah Bartmann) and the redirection of that eroticized gaze to white female bodies underscore the pervasive nineteenth-century male fear of cultural/racial dissolution embedded, as Sander Gilman has noted, in the act of miscegenation.[8] Bartmann will at every turn be represented as savage, primitive, foreign, grotesque, barbarous—a cultural and racial pariah, an enemy constructed by the French so as to be able "to exploit something ridiculous."

The vaudeville's opening scene is situated at the château of an aristocratic family just outside Paris. Hatred of Frenchwomen characterizes the sentiment of Adolph. *Femmephobia* is perhaps a more fitting description of Adolph's anxieties—he has a fear rather than a hatred of Frenchwomen. "Disgracefully deceived" by his first and second wives (7), he has sequestered himself at his uncle and aunt's château in the hope of avoiding the disarming charms of Frenchwomen. He envisions his next wife as "une exotique," "une sauvage" (7). His uncle, the baron, assures him that his extensive travel memoirs lead him to believe that only the beauty of "native American women and the Hottentots" rivals that of Frenchwomen (7). The baron's travel memoirs, however, do not extend beyond his imagination; he has never left France for these exotic places, nor has he seen these "wild" women. Rather, according to the baroness, "his imagination traveled for him" (6). The baron's imaginings, nonetheless, bring difference back (the unknown) into the familiar space of sameness by measuring the beauty of the "femmes sauvages" against familiar French frames of reference: the Françaises. We, the readers/audience, know Hottentot maidens and Indian squaws are beautiful because of their comparability to Frenchwomen, the embodiment of beauty itself.

The scene between the bumbling baron and the impressionable Adolph is immediately preceded by and juxtaposed to the scene between plotting-planning women: the baroness and Adolph's amorous, widowed cousin, Amelia. Amelia has secretly arrived at the château from Paris. The baroness explains to her niece that not only has Adolph "lost his mind," but he has "made a vow to only marry a woman absolutely foreign to our morals and customs" (3–5). Amelia's first response is one of incredulity, "You mean a savage?" (5), swiftly followed by a condemnation of Adolph's lack of "nationalist spirit" (5). To say that something is different from French customs and morals is to say that it is savage, Other, in this vaudeville. Adolph has "lost his mind," gone mad, gone primitive. He must be "cured of [his] madness" (31), for surely the desire for an Other woman is utter madness. His incomprehensible desires not only run counter to French ethnocentrism and racial hierarchization, but also deviate from the aristocracy's well-noted propensity for incestuous liaisons. Amelia will trick Adolph into marriage for his own happiness as well as to erase "all of [their] familial differences" (19). Difference must be suppressed culturally, racially, and familially.

The trickery takes the form of Amelia's impersonation of the Hottentot Venus, who is brought to her attention by a persistent suitor from Paris, the Chevalier d'Ericourt. Offering a lifetime of distractions, d'Ericourt shows her an advertisement for the most recent Parisian attraction: "A woman! This is a Venus, Madame! A Venus who has arrived here in France from England" (11). Bartmann is more than a woman; she is a Venus, the mythic goddess of beauty and sexuality. The Parisian women are so impressed with the Parisian men's admiration for the Hottentot that they "have already ordered dresses and overcoats in Hottentot styles" (12). The Hottentot Venus not only influences male sexual fantasy, but also feminine fashion for the "upcoming winter season" (12). Frenchwomen's desire to be desirable results in the appropriation of Bartmann's exhibition attire.

The chevalier continues with his backhanded recounting of the Venus's charms:

Really, this is no game!
Already all Paris praises her.

This woman is amazing:
First she speaks very little.
Her song seems barbarous,
Her dance is lively and burlesque,
Her face a little grotesque,
Her waist of a becoming contour.
One says that marriage binds her;
But this Venus, I wager,
Will never inspire love. (11)

The chevalier certainly cannot fathom Bartmann as an eroticized object of (white) male desire. The explicit reference to love and conjugal desire and "this Venus's" undesirability belie her designation as Venus. With her lively dance and primitive songs, she is diminished to a near-mute, entertaining spectacle for the French. Geographically, linguistically, culturally, and aesthetically, France, the French language, French culture, and Frenchwomen are privileged sites against which Bartmann, and hence Africa, are measured as primitive, savage, and grotesque.

Bartmann's symbolic presence acts as a mirror, legitimizing existing notions of the superiority of France and the inferiority of the Other. A savage and primitive image of Bartmann governs the piece. And as an image, she does not speak. She is, therefore, spoken for. The silent image (Bartmann) and the privileged voice (Amelia) are conflated. Amelia's knowledge of the "sauvage" allows her to represent the Hottentot Venus, Sarah Bartmann, and rename her Liliska. " 'Knowledge' involving the other is never objective, neutral, disinterested," writes critic Daniel Brewer, "insofar as the discourse of knowledge is inextricably bound up with the discourse of power." [9] To appropriate Bartmann's persona, to *re*-present her, is to, in Amelia's words, "perform a comedy" (12), to reduce Bartmann to an object of derision and thereby reveal her existence as comedic, and Adolph's desires for a "true savage" as laughable—a grotesque joke. The ease with which Amelia is able to perform as Bartmann brings to mind another artistic, literary motif and preoccupation popularized in the nineteenth century: white women as "closeted" sexual savages.

The comedic masquerade begins when the Frenchwoman figuratively in blackface and dressed *à la hottentote* is introduced to Adolph and the baron by the baroness. Liliska is a Hottentot from the "country of the Hottentots" (22). Adolph falls in love instantly with Liliska's exotic beauty. Yet a language barrier arises between the destined lovers. The well-traveled baron is asked to act as interpreter for Adolph. The baron improvises, inventing a language derived from French to communicate with the native:

Bellea Liliska, j'ea suisa votrea serviteura. Voulezi vousi répondrei ài l'amouri dei moni neveui. . . . C'est une langue mixte. Tous les sauvages . . . la comprennent. [Beautifula Liliska, Ia ama at youra servicea. Wouldi youi like to respondi toi myi nephewi's declarations of lovei. . . . It is a mixed language. All the savages . . . understand it.] (22)

All savages understand this mixed language, according to the baron, who makes no distinction between Hottentots and other "savages." Within this broadly defined category of indistinguishable savages are included Hottentots and the continuously mentioned Iroquois, as well as "all the savages from the Adriatic sea" (22). There is no difference between their cultures or languages. Possessing indiscriminate differences, savages become interchangeable; a savage is a savage is a savage.

Miming Bartmann, Liliska, the Hottentot, performs her trademark "barbarous" song and "burlesque" dance to impress her Parisian suitor:

Ric mir voulouf izami
Crif hec romir tonoe
Mar zemu *sambo* semi [emphasis mine]
Zang sir colofrinoc
Allious, Allious, allious, ou

Allious, nimou

Zic lomen coric zoni

Rif af volin olof

Trozalouf coric ani

Crouf ragoli riolof

Allious, allious, allious, ou

Allious, nimou. (24)

From these "neologisms," again articulated for comedic effect but at the same time representative of the native's difference, the word *sambo* glaringly stands out. Sambo was a popular American caricature of black men, one of the many ways in which white Americans desired to perceive black life. A jester of sorts, the Sambo image represented efforts "to make the black male into an object of laughter, and,

conversely, to force him to devise laughter, was to strip him of masculinity, dignity, and self-possession. Sambo was, then, an illustration of humor as a device of oppression, and one of the most potent in American popular culture. The ultimate objective for whites was to effect mastery: to render the black male powerless as a potential warrior, as a sexual competitor, as an economic adversary.[10]

Sambo's inclusion in this vaudeville is not gratuitous, nor a simple syntactic slip of the pen in mimicking the savage's tongue. Sambo's place of origin was seventeenth-century slave-trading Europe, specifically England. Like Bartmann, Sambo was imported to France from England via conceptualizations of Africa. The concept behind Sambo's creation — the use of humor as an oppressive device — is equally evident in this comedy. *The Hottentot Venus, or Hatred of Frenchwomen* is a caricature of Bartmann, an attestation of the way in which Parisians desired to construct not only Sarah Bartmann but all "savage women" as funny, primitive, but more important, inferior and ultimately sexually undesirable.

Liliska's soft-shoe routine rapidly brings us to the vaudeville's denouement. Adolph notes that were it not for Liliska's savage "candeur" and "innocence," he would have believed that she was a Frenchwoman:

You do not have at all
That strange and savage countenance of a country far away,
Your gaze is sweet and serene,
Grace animates your face.
Charming object, in truth,
If it were not for your candor, your innocence,
I would have believed, such is your beauty,
That your fatherland was France. (25)

Difference and sameness are thoroughly confounded in the vaudeville. Where there is stereotyped sameness (Frenchwomen's "serene gaze, beauty, grace"), the characters attempt to glean stereotyped difference (the savage's "candor and innocence"). And where there should be obvious difference, as in Amelia's usurpation of a black female identity, sameness emerges. Difference makes no difference at all, since the difference is always the same.

The moment of truth, the lifting of Amelia's primitive veil, arrives when the chevalier gallops in with a portrait of the real Hottentot Venus — Sarah Bartmann:

What a strange thing!
Such features until now unknown!
With such a face
She cannot be a Venus. (30) [11]

The baron then notices Amelia's same-difference: "I saw, however, that she did not have that swarthy complexion" (31).

Bartmann's "unknown features" do not conform to the French canon of feminine beauty. She is certainly not representative of the mythic Greek goddess of beauty and sexuality, and thus her billing as the Hottentot Venus is a misnomer.

"It is, undoubtedly with derision," wrote Professor Verneau, "that she was nicknamed the Hottentot Venus." [12] She is, rather, a hideous mirror, a "grotesque spectacle," that legitimizes French aesthetics of beauty and cultural norms, that reinscribes Frenchwomen as "objets charmants." Adolph's jungle fever is remedied with a dose of "effrayante" Hottentot reality. The Manichaean world, the dialectics of superiority (France) and inferiority (Africa), is left wholly intact. The gulf between black and white, between "Hottentot" and French, between civilization and the jungle, is unbridgeable. The seriousness of the investigation, the occasional "reality check" of one's footing as superior, was carried out under the facade of humor. *The Hottentot Venus, or Hatred of Frenchwomen,* like Balzac's *La Fille aux yeux d'or,*[13] opens with a show of reverence for exotic difference and ends literally in incestuous sameness: Adolph and Amelia are united in marital bliss—members of the same race, culture, nationality, and family.

3

"The Other Woman": Reading a Body

of Difference in Balzac's *La Fille aux yeux d'or*

What is woman? A little thing, a bundle of nonsense.
— Balzac, *La Fille aux yeux d'or*

In his undelivered lecture entitled "Femininity," Freud ventured to decipher what no man before him had ever successfully discerned — the nature of femininity:

To-day's lecture, too, should have no place in an introduction. . . . It brings forward nothing but observed facts, almost without any speculative additions. . . . Throughout history people have knocked their heads against the riddle of femininity. . . . Nor will you have escaped worrying over this problem — those of you who are men; to those of you who are women, this will not apply — you are yourselves the problem.[1]

Freud's inquiry reflects the tendency of Western patriarchal discourse to render unintelligible and incomprehensible peoples and cultures that do not conform to the normative gaze. The lecture "Femininity" is an attempt to capture "Woman" through observation and in writing in order to make her more accessible to the people who have knocked their heads against her riddled nature — men. And while the late psychoanalyst maintains that his work offers no speculative additions, "Femininity" is pure speculation, a specularizing, or mirroring project/projection that uses the masculine as its point of departure to discern the nature of the feminine.

And since Freud never discovered the nature of the feminine, some forty-two years later a rereading of "Femininity" was undertaken by one of its objects of inquiry, Luce Irigaray, in *Speculum de l'autre femme*. Irigaray determines that woman, as she exists in phallocentric thought, is a lesser man with the clitoral equivalent of the penis. Woman is defined by male subjects, by male parameters. In this specular logic of sameness, the masculine is mediated through the feminine; femininity is repressed, erased. And the nature of femininity that Freud found so puzzling and analyzed in "unfriendly" terms is the result of woman's position as "a disadvantaged little man, a more narcissistic, little man because of the mediocrity of her genital organ." [2]

In both the writings of Freud and Irigaray a particular erasure and universality occurs. If Freud privileges white male hegemony, Irigaray privileges a white female hegemony — indeed, one could argue a privileging of a particular class as well. Certainly, the opportunity to observe the nature of the "other woman" did not present itself to Freud in Austria — nor perhaps was the subject of particular importance. And in her otherwise insightful critique, Irigaray sets up the very logic of sameness against which she argues. Her repressed woman becomes the universal body that defines all female experiences. White femaleness and maleness dominate both economies of representation. The Freudian question, "What does femininity mean for men?" and the Irigarayan rereading, "What does femininity for men mean for women?" ask in reality: "What does white femininity mean for white men?" and "What does white femininity for white men mean for white women?"

What are the implications for nonwhite women of this politics of domination? Are they even lesser men, lesser beings (slaves even) than white women by virtue of their racial and sexual difference? "What does Other femininity for white men mean for Other women?" It is precisely this polemic that I wish to take up in a reading of the erotic Balzacian narrative *La Fille aux yeux d'or,* whose female protagonist, Paquita Valdès, functions as a racial and sexual Other and a slave.

Considerable attention has been given to the themes of orientalism and the questions of sex and class differences in Balzac's short tale, at the expense of a rigorous analysis of the racial difference that manifests itself in the body of the female protagonist. Generally, the category of race has understandably been analyzed along the lines of Balzac's *rêveries orientales,* or neatly subsumed into a reading of sex and class differences (that is, master and slave, man and woman), without taking into consideration the vertible socioeconomic and political differences between a slave woman and a woman who is not a slave. I would argue that Paquita's sex "and" race are intimately linked to her position as slave. The differences between white femininity and Other femininity, between woman and racialized slave woman, between Euphémie and Paquita, become deftly apparent at the novel's tragic end. Yet in a novella rampant with what Doris Kadish calls "hybrids," [3] the erasure of race may stem perhaps from the ambiguity emanating from the text itself.

Situating Paquita is somewhat frustrated by a very fluid Balzacian cartography that traverses countries (France, Spain, Cuba, England, Georgia) and cultures. Her mysterious origins begin with her denatured mother—a slave woman bought in "Géorgie" for her rare beauty. Georgia's Eurasian locale points back to the all-too-well-noted oriental bent of the text. Racial difference inserts itself immediately with Balzac's description of the mother as possessing "to the highest degree that gravity akin to savage races" (375).[4] In Balzac's tediously class-delineated Paris (according to those who have gold [*l'or*] and those who don't), it is only fitting that distinctions be drawn between civilized and savage races, between European and Eurasian stock, between Western and Eastern cultures. Cultural differences are perceived as concrete racial differences. Paquita is a slave because of her mother's racial/cultural differences. Yet her racial otherness is also manifested outside of orientalism.

Alternately referred to as "Spaniard" (372), "the unknown" (351), and "a young creole from the Antilles" (343), Paquita presents a tropical disruption to orientalist readings. She is, in a word, Other, a body of utter difference: "Asiatic through her mother, European through education, Tropical through birth" (388).

A Creole, from the Spanish *criollo*, or *criar*, which means to breed, or nurture, is a person of European descent born especially in the West Indies or Spanish America. According to the *Grand Larousse de la langue française* (1972), *Creole* was also used to differentiate New World blacks, that is, blacks born in the New World from Africans newly imported to the colonies. Creolization, thus, describes European and African naturalization in the New World; creolity, then, is a purely geographic marker. Yet the nineteenth-century discourse on creolity in the *Larousse du XIXème siècle* is clearly racialized:

It is in the large lively eyes of creole women that one finds that especially rare contrast of sweet languor and striking vivacity. They are particularly distinguishable by their beautiful hair, which is incomparably black, and by the smallness of their arched feet. . . . Their limbs are almost always endowed with a suppleness that makes them eminently suitable for all bodily exercises. . . . The only difference between them [the blacks] and white creoles consists in skin color and hair texture.

By drawing on physical and emotional specificities, and, therefore, distinctions from the French born in France and similarities between Caribbean-born blacks, the process of creolization is racialized. Creoles appear to be a separate, distinct race formed on the basis of their colonial experiences. The "white" Creole is, in fact, biracial. These biracial characteristics are exhibited in the Creole woman in particular. Suppleness of the body, small, arched feet, and incomparably dark, beautiful hair distinguish the Creole woman from the French woman. With the black woman the Creole shares culture, nationality, and geographic space. Even her gaze represents a rare contrast—biraciality: blackness = languor and whiteness = vivacity.

In *Curiosités esthétiques*, Baudelaire also evokes the biracial gaze in his description of the Creole poet Leconte de Lisle.[5] The exoticism, timelessness, and sensuality—the blackness—associated with the colonies envelop the Creole woman and filter osmotically into her blood. Blackness is like a contagion contracted through proximity. The whiteness of flesh and texture of hair constitute her only distinctions from her black female counterpart.

The "particularly distinguishing" attributes of the Larousse's *femme créole* are strikingly consonant with those of *The Girl with the Golden Eyes*. Balzac pays particular tribute to Paquita's "pied bien attaché, mince, recourbé" (353) and "beaux cheveux noirs" (375). Paquita's creolity marks her racial alterity, her biraciality. In his description of Paquita, Henri de Marsay evokes this two-ness: "This girl resembles a cat that wants to rub against your legs, a girl white as ashes, delicate in appearance . . . but within her movements passion slumbers. . . . This is an ideal woman" (351–52, 383). A dichotomy is drawn between Paquita's appearance and her sexual nature. She is at once white and delicate in appearance, yet bestial and sexual. Her contrasted slumbering, voluptuous nature and beautifully placid white exterior coincide with the romantic discourse on the *mulâtresse:*

Admirable for some, criminal for others, the Mulâtresse will become one of the major figures of romantic eros. . . . [she has a] reputation for beauty, reputation for immorality equally. The lascivious sensuality of the blacks flows within their veins, but they are refined by their whiteness. . . . The Mulâtresse is the proposed ideal mistress of the erotic imagination of the average Frenchman.[6]

Both the Creole and the mulâtresse are white, yet inescapably black, and thus unable to shake the lascivious and ardent stereotypes of black female sexuality.

The French conceptualizations of the femme créole and the mulâtresse are virtually interchangeable:

Mulâtresse	Négresse[7]	Paquita
black and white	black	white
lascivious	lascivious	supple
voluptuous	voluptuous	voluptuous
sensuality	sensuality	abyss of pleasures
animality	animality	animality
languor	languor	languor
ardent	ardent	ardent
immorality	immorality	
beauty		beauty
ideal		ideal

It is from the sexually racialized stereotypes of the *Négresse* that the sexual nature of both the mulatto woman and the Creole woman are conceived. The Négresse is not ideal; she does not represent beauty, but rather sexuality. The canon of feminine beauty is constructed around whiteness, while voluptuous sexuality is mysterious, dark — black. In a Pygmalion-like fashion, two erotic, exotic, and idyllic forms of femininity are created from the Négresse and white femaleness.

Physically white, and simultaneously epitomizing racial difference, Paquita, like the mulâtresse of the nineteenth century, is indeed de Marsay's ideal mistress:

Last Thursday . . . I found myself face to face with a woman. . . . My dear friend, physically speaking, this incognita is the most adorably feminine woman I have ever met. . . . And what most struck me, that with which I am still captivated, is her two eyes, yellow as those of a tiger's; a golden yellow that gleams, enlivened gold . . . amorous gold that wants to come into your waistcoat. . . . Since I have begun to contemplate women, my unknown is the only one whose virginal bosom, whose ardent and voluptuous curves have realized for me the unique woman of my dreams. . . . She is an ideal woman, an abyss of pleasures where one wallows endlessly . . . this is an ideal woman whom one sees rarely in France. . . . I must have this girl for a mistress. (351–52, 364)

Paquita is the essence of feminine sensuality and beauty: an exotic beauty that evokes purity, on the one hand, with her "virginal bosom," and voluptuousness, on the other, signified by her "ardent curves." She is white and black in the flesh; she is ideal.

Henri desires to possess the girl with the golden eyes, to become the slave woman's master and to master her sexually. Desire is fundamentally the narcissistic drive to impose oneself on another and to be recognized by the Other.[8] Henri clearly imposes/projects himself onto Paquita: "Frankly speaking, from the expression on her face, she seemed to be saying: 'What! you are here, my ideal, the being of my thoughts, of my dreams. . . . Take me, I am yours. . .'" (351). Paquita not only "recognizes" Henri, but begs that he take possession of her. She is reduced to a mere object: the object of Henri's sexual desires, but equally an object to be possessed—a slave woman. And as a slave, Henri's "plaything" (396), she has no will, desire, or subjectivity other than to be "a pleasure" for Henri (398). Void of subjectivity, a sort of blank object awaiting inscription, Paquita is invested with masculine desire. Her desires are those of Henri, the master, the white male.

And Henri, a fop par excellence, must "live and sleep in front of a mirror."[9] Paquita is that mirror. Paquita is *plaisir* and *or*, a never-ending harvest of rich, sensual self-indulgence and reflexivity. She is "nature's work of art" (368), created to sexually satiate and envelop him, and to constantly reflect and recognize his idealized self-image.

Henri's quest for this mirroring abyss of perfection is realized with the help of the Othello-like *mulâtre* Christemio, Paquita's "foster father" (376). The mulatto surrogate father further colors Paquita's Creole origins. Balzac's portraiture of Christemio is rather generous in its use of racialized language:

Never has an African figure better expressed such breadth of vengeance, quickness of suspicion, promptness within the execution of a thought, the strength of the Moor, and his childlike irreflection. His dark eyes had the fixity of a bird of prey . . . like those of a vulture. His forehead, small and low, had something of a menacing nature. (366)

In uncanny Gobineauesque language,[10] Balzac credits the black with irreflection, a void of intellect. From Christemio's physiognomy — "small and low forehead" — Balzac reads his emotional and mental capacity. Propelled by violent, hasty emotions and vengeance rather than calculated rational thoughts, like Shakespeare's Othello the Moor, Christemio is a sheer brute of a man, a black beast, in his use of strength to compensate for his "childlike" impulsiveness.

His presence in the text is not only symbolic of Paquita's alterity but a cliché. If one reads *La Fille aux yeux d'or* as an orientalist text, Christemio functions as a eunuch, the castrated attendant in feminine bed chambers. However, if one reads against the grain of orientalism and pushes this creolized reading further, Christemio would appear to serve as a reminder of the primitive sensuality of the colonies. He represents the contagious blackness that has osmotically filtered into the Creole woman's blood, the "slumbering passion" that lurks in Paquita's movements. He is an exotic backdrop, thrice used to take Henri to his out-of-this world, dreamlike sexual experience.[11] The possibility of Henri's sexual gratification is mediated through Christemio, his "guide" to the "unique woman of his dreams" (369), to the abyss of sexual pleasures. And as Henri navigates his way to Paquita through Christemio, he experiences the sensation of being in an Ann Radcliffe novel, "where the hero crosses cold, somber, uninhabited rooms, of some melancholy and deserted place" (369). Blackness is the primal, since it is only through the black — Christemio — that sexual gratification can be realized.

True to form, during the two love scenes, Paquita invites Henri into her "Venus's shell" (369), and she takes him "upon her wings, transporting him to the seventh heaven of love" (394). However, during the last celestial sexual encounter, Paquita exclaims in ecstasy, "Mariquita" (401).[12] The fop is brought abominably low; "his manly pride" is usurped not by another man but by a woman (401). At this moment of emasculation, effeminization, Henri vows to kill Paquita.

Rather than reexplore the overwrought, but nonetheless accurate, readings of the triangularity encoded in the names Mariquita, Paquita, and Henri de Marsay, lesbianism and the ambiguous sexuality present in the name Euphémie Porrabéril, Paquita's use as a mask for the incestuous relationship between the half-brother and sister, Henri and Euphémie, and Henri's clearly effeminate beauty and resemblance to his sister, which led to Paquita's misnaming, I will move directly to the tragic denouement where the meaning of Other femininity is disclosed.

Viciously murdered by the jealously enraged marquise for her sexual indiscretion, Paquita lies drowning in her own blood. The dagger in her hand still dripping with fresh blood, the marquise looks up to find Henri. This scene of recognition is followed by the mutual affirmation of common paternity—Lord Dudley. Henri, wounded by Paquita's emasculating infidelity, points to the expiring slave woman and declares: "Elle était fidèle au sang." This critical sentence has been translated and interpreted as, "She was faithful to the bloodlines," that is, she was attracted to the brother and sister, the same blood.[13] Yet this same sentence has also been translated as, "She was true to the instincts of her race."[14] The latter translation best captures Paquita's exchangeability and disposability as a slave woman. In essence, Paquita is like all the others; void of subjectivity, she is commodified into a prototypical specimen of her race, a stereotyped being "true to the instincts of her race."[15]

Reduced to a generic, racially stereotyped object, Paquita can be exchanged for any "Other slave Woman." This commodification is further revealed by Euphémie when Dona Concha sees her daughter's ravaged body: "You are going to tell me that you did not sell her in order for me to kill her. . . . I know why you have come out of your den. I will pay you a second time for her" (406). Paquita, whose death is redeemable for gold, is a lesser being, a lesser woman, because of her racial and sexual Otherness, which translates into her subjugation, and thus enslaved objectification and unscrupulous murder. She is, as Doris Kadish relates, "a non-being.[16] Exchangeability and disposability seem to accurately define the meaning of Other femininity for Balzac.[17] Yet the veritable unveiling of the meaning of 'Other femininity' begins with de Marsay's contemptuous response to the riddle of femininity: "Et qu'est-ce que la femme? Une petite chose, un ensemble de niaiseries" (And what is woman? A little thing, a bundle of nonsense) (360). Woman is a little thing, a bundle of absurdities, "twaddle," silliness; woman simply makes no sense; she is non-sense.

If woman is but a little thing, what of the Other woman? This non-rhetorical question brings us to Balzac's pronouncement on woman: "Woman and paper are two white things that suffer everything."[18] As Peter Brooks has remarked, the statement implies that woman, like paper, is written/inscribed upon by men.[19] The male writer's pen penetrates the page and the woman, thus marking both. Woman suffers penetration/inscription. But, more important, woman is white. The "Other woman" does not exist for Balzac. She is less than a little thing, therefore, invisible, nothing, a no-thing. And when she attempts to rear her quintessentially different head, to articulate desire outside of the dominant economy of representation, and thus subjectivity, she is physically suppressed, bludgeoned out of existence. In sum, the combination of racial and sexual Otherness in this erotic novella is deadly.

4

Black Blood, White Masks, and Négresse Sexuality

in de Pons's *Ourika, l'Africaine*

The Europeans in general and the French in particular, not satisfied with simply ignoring the Negro of the colonies, repudiate the one whom they have shaped into their own image. —René Maran, *Un Homme pareil aux autres*

Perhaps no other nineteenth-century French novel spawned more offshoots than Mme. Claire de Duras's *Ourika*. Published in 1823, *Ourika* inspired novellas of the same title or derivatives such as *La nouvelle Ourika, ou les avantages de l'éducation; Ourika, ou l'orpheline africaine;* performance pieces; literary criticism by Sainte-Beuve; and poetry.

Ourika is based on the story of a real-life Ourika who was purchased as a gift for the Duchess of Orléans by a colonial administrator of Senegal, the Chevalier de Boufflers, in or around 1788.[1] In his journal, he wrote of his purchase of the slave girl, who would become, some thirty-six years later, immortalized in Duras's novella: "I am buying at this moment a little Négresse of two or three years of age in order to send her to Madame the Duchess of Orléans. . . . I feel myself brought to tears in thinking that this poor child has been sold to me like a little lamb."[2] Ourika died at the tender age of sixteen of a mysterious illness. The Duchess of Orléans's little *Négresse* provided lively conversation in the salons of nineteenth-century Paris where Boufflers's letters were read. And these "lively" conversations provided fodder for Claire de Duras's fictional Ourika.

In Duras's story, the Senegalese girl is brought to France as a gift to an aristocratic woman, Madame de B. Afforded all the privileges and the breeding of women of her class, Ourika experiences a profound alienation and malaise instigated by "a conversation, overheard by chance, [which] opened [her] eyes and ended [her] youth" (198).[3] Ourika learns that she is a Negress, that she is afflicted with "blackness." An unrequited interracial love story is equally intertwined. Ourika is in love with Madame de B's grandson, Charles. Yet her hopes for love are quickly dashed because of their unrealizability (owing to her malediction). As Madame de B's confidante, Madame de— matter-of-factly says: "Who will want to marry a Negress?" (199).

Ourika's situation is strikingly similar to that of protagonist Jean Veneuse, of René Maran's semi-autobiographical *Un Homme pareil aux autres,* who was diagnosed by Fanon in *Black Skin, White Masks* as an abandonment-neurotic. One can easily substitute the pronouns, proper names, adjectives, and places of birth—*she* for *he, Negress* for *Negro, Ourika* for *Jean, Senegal* for the *Antilles*—in Fanon's analysis of Veneuse's crisis and arrive at the same abject conclusion: "[Ourika] is a [Negress]. Born in [Senegal], [she] has lived in [Paris] for years; so [she] is European. But [she] is black; so [she] is a [Negress]. There is the conflict."[4] Ironically, the process of substituting one black body for another as a function of colonialist discourse will be revisited in our inquiry. Ourika, like Veneuse, cannot escape her corporeality and all that blackness signifies. However, our heroine's plight is especially burdensome, particularly when gender and the question of slavery are factored into the racial equation.

Since Ourika is destined to want only those men who will never want her, that is, aristocratic white men, and is "unable to be assimilated, unable to go unnoticed,"[5] her spinsterlike future is sealed; she can never marry, and thus exiles herself to the convent, joining other unmarried and unmarriageable women. She cannot, as her benevolent benefactress, Madame de B, suggests, "rise above her position," for to do so would "breach the natural order of things" (199). Ourika's presence as a free Négresse defies the fate of perpetual servitude reserved for blacks during the ancien régime. Slavery and blackness were naturalized, synonymous, just as whiteness and mastery were, and no amount of education would "allow her to rise above her position," would white-out Ourika's blackness.

Although it is a sympathetic and insightful critique of race, sex, and class politics in eighteenth-century France, Mme. Claire de Duras's *Ourika* is not of particular interest here except as a point of departure and comparison. Rather, it is the Count Gaspard de Pons's elegy *Ourika, l'Africaine* that specifically relates to our discussion. Written in 1825, two years after the publication of Duras's novel, *Ourika, l'Africaine* is the last elegy in de Pons's compilation of poetry entitled *Inspirations poètiques*.[6] The romantic poet offers a brief preface and dedication before each of his poems. *Ourika, l'Africaine* is dedicated to a Monsieur Charles Nodier.

Charles Nodier was a nineteenth-century writer whose article on slavery in the French colonies, "De l'esclavage," appeared in the *L'Observateur des colonies*. Nodier's position on slavery is somewhat ambiguous, for he, on the one hand, condemns the institution because of its immorality and, on the other, absolves the colonialists of their deeds because of the inherent inferiority and vileness of the blacks, who desperately need civilizing. Images of the rebellion of Saint Domingue (Haiti) in 1791, where the French were slaughtered by the "evil" black "savages," still plagued the French psyche into the nineteenth century.[7]

Nodier's teetering position reflects the tensions of many a nineteenth-century French citizen. Slavery was so tied to French economic prosperity that the thought of abolishing the system was, to say the least, disturbing. Indeed, the system was abolished in 1791, only to be reestablished by Napoleon. The moral implications of the institution proved as weighty a consideration, for it was philosophe Montesquieu who wrote in an irony-laden tone a little more than a half century earlier in *Spirit of the Laws:* "It is impossible for us to assume that these people are men because if we assumed that they were men one would begin to believe that we ourselves were not Christians." [8] But whether the French were pro-slavery, anti-slavery, or merely ambivalent, blacks and their site of difference, blackness, were systematically represented as savage, cruel, bestial, and sexual. And these are the sentiments that rang out clearly in Nodier's writing, and that de Pons seems to have shared.

Yet de Pons's "poetic inspiration" for *Ourika, l'Africaine,* which is disclosed in the preface, is even more revealing than the dedication. He specifically mentions the "charming elegy," *Ourika,* written in 1824 by Mme. Emile de Girardin, née Delphine Gay. Gay's poem, dedicated to "Madame La Duchesse de Duras," remains truer to the original writer's vision; it is a depiction of the suffering Senegalese muse replete with the themes of denied motherhood, unrequited love, humility, and, more than any of these, piety.[9] Distraught over her repudiation, this Ourika nonetheless finds solace in death as a Christian.

Gaspard de Pons insists that his version merely elaborates on aspects of the muse's character that the woman writer, prevented by her sex and inexperience, was forbidden to imagine. And as an experienced man of letters released from biological and social constraints, such as those surrounding the imagining of sexualized black female bodies, he would present an authentic portraiture.

De Pons's elegy begins with a tormented Ourika who is cognizant of her racial difference. Gone is the sad, unrequited love story. Gone is the self-deprecating, victimized Ourika. De Pons projects a sexualized narrative onto the black female body which uses the intersection of race and sex as tropes to unveil the Négresse's "natural" differences, reified in stereotypes of lascivious sexuality, jealousy, and savagery. Notwithstanding his protagonist's French education and refinements, de Pons's *Ourika, l'Africaine* reminds its readers that French hierarchies and prejudices are in order, as Ourika's differences are fetishized and imagined as a magical essence in the blood.[10]

Négresse Sexuality

The Négresse is pivotal to any discussion of black female sexuality as well as the sexual propensities of her diaspora—the Créole, the *mulâtresse,* the octoroon, the quadroon, and so on—in the nineteenth century; she is foundational, thus representing sheer blackness, unadultered sexuality, pure Africa.

Blackness and beauty were antithetical in nineteenth-century France. Accordingly, the Negress was generally stereotypically conceived as unaesthetically pleasing with her "dark skin," "large lips," "flat nose," and "frizzy hair," unless she was physiognomically overlaid with whiteness and transformed into a Négresse blanche/white-Negro woman.[11] The lure of the négresse, then, was her adeptness at sexual arts. She epitomized Black Venus. Her lure was loathed also, for she represented danger, a sexual passion capable of satiation and consumption, the literal siphoning off of life through the draining of precious seminal liquor. As bell hooks writes, "Encounters with Otherness are clearly marked as more exciting, more intense, more threatening. The lure is pleasure and danger."[12]

Thus de Pons's Ourika will be at once desired and feared, exciting and overwhelming, all too willing to satiate her beloved white male, and to seek retribution if he rejects her offerings. Unlike Claire de Duras's and Delphine Gay's Ourika, this Ourika will not quietly suffer her pariah state. She removes the white mask, allowing "the blood of Othello" to propel her to seek passion and vengeance (223).

Colonialist Prototypes/Stereotypes

De Pons's poetic rendition further epitomizes obsessions of a romantic imagination shot through with a phantasmal, colonialist discourse. The added *Africaine* in the title conspicuously recalls and reinforces a host of popular primitive images of the black, from sexual savages to bestial brutes. The "the" rather than "an" points

to a colonialist stratagem that attempts to rid the "Other" of his—
or her, in this case—subjectivity. Ourika is the quintessential African female; she is Africa; she is a prototype, a sign of difference that
will be made culturally and racially productive.

The Black Venus narrative, a function of the overarching Afri-
canist/colonialist discursive system, allows de Pons to negotiate "in
the blood" distinctions between the African female Other and the
French male self, between Europe and Africa, France and Senegal. Ourika will be incorporated productively into this dialectic as
evil, primitive, sexual, mad, as a subjugated "Other" who will affirm
French identity, culture, and normativity.

Another stratagem of colonialist discourse is the trope of pro-
sopopoeia,[13] or the act of putting words into the Negress's mouth,
thereby giving "active presence," as observed by Barthes, and authenticity to the absence or incorporeality involved in the process
of representing the Other. It will be from the mouth of the Negress
that we learn of the African's savagery and inferiority.

Ourika, l'Africaine opens with the heroine/narrator "alone in bed
as daybreak appears" (218). She has overheard the revelatory exchange between Madame de B and Madame de—. She contemplates
rising to look at the glacial sky in her adopted homeland and dreams
of the warmth of Africa, thus offering up the binary oppositions of
hot/cold, Africa/Europe, Senegal/France, nature/culture, sexu-
ality/frigidity, rationality/irrationality:

> There, under the sun, nature takes over
> Makes man brave the calm of the deserts,
> Crying wild from love to which he submits to chains
> It is lightning here; there, it is fire. (218)

Africa is a primitive utopia of free-flowing sexuality where ecstatic sexual encounters are infinite and celebrated with bestial cries.
Sexual pleasure is as brusque and infinitesimal in Europe as it is fiery
and endless in Africa. Europe literally and figuratively pales in comparison to Africa's primitivism.

Ourika is pulled from her celestial reverie with the realization that she has been duped, denied her passionate birthright for an elusive French identity:

> I have brought this fervor to these icy climates,
> Where my appearance alone declares that I am a stranger there;
> The whites have taught me their lying virtue,
> Which cannot contain my mad desires.
>
> . . . .
>
> Ah! How it serves me, me, this austere modesty,
> Of which one took much care to surround my childhood?
> The flame that embraces me has the right to tame it.
> That I bend to your laws my devouring ecstasy,
> Am I less in your eyes, am I but a Negress? (218–20)

Ourika was given to Madame de B to mold like a soft wax figurine into a *noble* savage. However, the benefactress's attempts to erase Ourika's difference have failed dismally, for the African woman now understands that her difference, her less-than-ness, continuously manifests itself in her corporeality. Even more inflammatory to the African heroine is the fact that her quest for feminine *pudeur,* her mimicry of French women's modesty, has not served her at all. She is still less: a négresse. There is no identification—only profound difference.

As her lamentations progress, Ourika's discourse becomes more feverish and sexualized. She sheds her pudeur, allowing the hitherto repressed, intoxicating African "flame" to consume it. Ourika beckons her beloved to satiate her, offering "Other-worldly" gratifications in return:

> Flee your women from the North whose coldness outrages me;
> Come, Charles! In our gazes, in the desert of my homeland,
> A green oasis offers itself, that the colossal tree,
> The vast baobab shades with its branches.
> Here, one hundred black beauties will come to seduce your favor;
> It is me who will please you, because I am the most beautiful. (220–21)

The voyage to Ourika's Africa is an exotic one that offers entry into a dreamworld of pleasures. De Pons envisions an Africa populated with oases, baobabs, and a harem of black beauties, fertile refuges, waiting to please the reticent white male.

Ourika's offerings are unintelligible to Charles—simply beyond his comprehension and the realm of French male imagination. This incomprehensibility is implicitly racial. He cannot see Ourika's African beauty; it is foreign, strange, Other—not French, not normative. This blindness incites the muse's rage. She rhapsodizes on the historic uses and abuses of black women by Europeans during the slave trade:

> The African woman, sold for the pleasures of white men,
> Within the arms of a tyrant who disdains her,
> Her own pleasures vainly neglected,
> Mad intoxication from his burning kisses. (221)

The European slave trade, a system based on conquests and exploitation of "Other" bodies and lands, is here romanticized. Rape is romanticized and sexual coercion erased. The bodies of black women have been commodified into resources for white male pleasure. As sex objects/sex slaves, black women are complicitous in their sexual commodification, enjoying the "burning kisses" of men who disdain, sexploit, and enslave them.

In the following stanza of the elegy, Ourika again beckons Charles to "open [your] arms for me, savage!" (221). She begs for fulfillment, sexual (mis)use. But Charles, unlike his barbarous brethren, does not accede. He has eyes only for French, that is, "white," beauty—Anais, Ourika's "eternal rival" (222).

The sexually depraved African then cautions: "Fear me, Charles, Fear me. . . . /I am still, however, the child of my country" (222). Ourika gradually doffs every learned French moral, refinement, and modesty, until one is faced with her utter African womanness. Africa has been unearthed, uncloaked, and French repudiation is legitimized. The "real" Ourika is a frothing at-the-mouth, raving, sexual savage:

> Be cautious in provoking some African wraths!
> You talk of friendship, of this weak bond
> Which breaks a jealous heart hardly known to yours!
> The blood of Othello flows always in my veins.
>
> Suffering exhausts me, I need remorse;
> A crime means nothing to me, nothing, if it is revenge.
> . . . Do I not hear your indulgent God?
> O rage! he forbids murder and death. (223)

Black blood is ever present. Geographic boundaries are collapsed. Africa represents one large mass of black, passionate, vengeful Othellos and Ourikas. Ourika is not only jealous and sexualized, but an infidel whose barbarous proclivities predispose her to transgressive, impious thoughts. Mourning the loss of love offers the black female savage no consolation. She must avenge herself. In spite of her fear of the European God's thunder and prohibition of murder (223), Ourika turns her wrath to the innocent Anais. Like the barbarian Saint Dominguans of the first *Ourika*, she imagines "slitting" the white woman's throat in a fit of jealous passion (223).

"Ferocity remains a dominant characteristic of the black soul," writes Hoffmann, "[and] writers of the romantic period abundantly illustrated the savagery of Africans."[14] Black femininity and white femininity are as implicitly contrasted as Africa and Europe are explicitly compared. One envisions a wild-eyed black woman, driven by her disorderly sex and black blood, heinously murdering the uncompromisingly modest white woman. As in Balzac's *La Fille aux yeux d'or*, this utter difference must be exiled, purged. And Ourika's exile results in a metaphoric, violent death and a descent into hell.

By the elegy's end, our heroine begs forgiveness. She imagines herself now brutally stabbed to death ("poignardée") by Charles for her impetuousness:[15]

From the laws of modesty when I dare to free myself,
It is in secret; pardon my burning audacity.
For my color I must also ask forgiveness:
If I do not blush, it is because I cannot blush.

And from your hand I must die stabbed,
I would not feel the horror of the fatal blow
Within this burning happiness which seems hardly evil,
Within the swelter of fire in which I die inundated. (224)

Ourika's ranting, feverish tone is abruptly halted. The mask of whiteness, of French culture, is again donned. Our heroine is penitent and apologetic with regard to her blackness, which prevents her from visibly manifesting shame. Again, Ourika's difference rears its black head.

But there is no forgiveness for the heathenish African heroine who dons and doffs French masks like hats. That blackness and evil are equated in the French imagination is deftly apparent as Ourika is sentenced to purgatory. In a quasi-Baudelairian descent into the depths of hell, the black woman finds solace, a reconciliation of the tormented self. She welcomes her death as a sort of deliverance, preferring to die violently at the hands of her beloved than to die from the agony of his unreturned love.

De Pons's clichéd elegy elicits stereotype after stereotype of Négresse sexuality, Africa, blackness, and black blood. French culture cannot tame the laws of nature that govern the African woman. Africa is always somehow lurking in the recesses. Geographic displacements are fleeting, and European education is at best an elusive stopgap.

Indeed, one cannot take Africa out of the African woman; it is in her blood.

5

Black Is the Difference: Identity, Colonialism,

and Fetishism in *La Belle Dorothée*

Because of its systematic negation of the other person . . . colonialism forces the people it dominates to ask themselves the question constantly: "In reality, who am I?"—Frantz Fanon, *The Wretched of the Earth*

Besides Pierre Loti, perhaps the nineteenth-century French writer best known for his flirtations with the exotic is poet Charles-Pierre Baudelaire. Baudelaire's well-documented, stormy affair with a mulatto prostitute, Jeanne Duval, and his travels to France's tropical colonies in the years of 1841–42 serve as the subject matter for a number of Baudelaire's poems and as the well of much literary criticism and many biographies. *La Vénus noire* cycle, or the Jeanne Duval poems, from Baudelaire's once-censored *Les Fleurs du mal* (20–35), as this collection of poems have come to be popularly known, are distinguishable primarily because of the poet's never-ending references to the most important signifier of Jeanne's difference—her color:

> Upon this fawn and brownish complexion makeup was superb
> It flushed with blood this skin the color of amber! (20)
>
> Bizarre deity, dark as the nights
> Witch with ebony flanks, child of black midnights. (24)[1]

Indeed, blackness for Baudelaire epitomizes the exotic.[2] Yet the fixation on blackness, particularly the musings on Black Venus, are not unique to the Jeanne Duval cycle. Baudelaire's *La Belle Dorothée* (whose principal personage, Dorothée, is a black prostitute), which is included in his compilation of prose poems, *Petits poèmes en prose*,[3] should be considered in any perusal of Baudelairian exoticism. However, our primary interest here relates to the larger sociohistorical and cultural issues of nineteenth-century colonialism, fetishism, identity, and prostitution in the prose poem.

Although nineteenth-century France witnessed the dawning of racial-sexual science and the rehashing of the doctrine of the great chain of being, which situated Europeans at the center and Africans at the margins of evolution, the eighteenth century had in fact laid the groundwork for such discussions of identity and difference with the French slave trade, colonialism, and the legacy of historiographical travelogues like Bougainville's *Voyage autour du monde*, which provided French readers with imaginative accounts of exotic lands and savage people. Counted among the more extensive, well respected, and often cited of these resources by scientific successors such as naturalist Georges Cuvier, was a travel journal published in 1790, *Voyage dans l'intérieur de l'Afrique*. This ethnographic text, replete with lithographs, described the flora and fauna of South Africa, including the inhabitants of Kaffraria, who were predominantly Khoikhoi and often referred to as Kaffirs or Caffres as well as Hottentots in early travel literature. The Khoikhoi females' notoriety, as we have seen, was derived from their steatopygia and the famous *apron* worn around their waists to cover their fabled privates. The author of this travel book was naturalist François Le Vaillant, the great-uncle of Charles Baudelaire.

Contained within the pages of Le Vaillant's *Voyage* is a lithograph entitled "Femme caffre." The sketch features a topless African woman wearing an apron and holding an infant. At the tender age of thirteen, Baudelaire requested a copy of *Voyage dans l'intérieur de l'Afrique* in a letter to his mother, Caroline Archimbaut-

Dufays.[4] More than simply demonstrating an eyebrow-raising familial preoccupation with exotica—specifically, black female bodies—the sketch may have duly impressed the aspiring poet, for some twenty-seven years later *La Belle Dorothée* appeared in Baudelaire's *Poèmes en prose,* and the muse and her female compatriots are curiously referred to as Cafrines in the prose poem, a possible feminine derivative of Caffres.[5]

The Hottentot Apron, Fetishization, and the Prostitute

During the nineteenth century there was a marked increase in participation by domestic workers—*les bonnes* and *femmes de chambres,* for example—in sexually venal activities within the bourgeois households of Paris. Tales of maids of easy virtue populated the novels of the frères Goncourts, Octave Mirbeau, and Guy de Maupassant. Of the popularity of the maid servant and her association with sexual vice and venality, Alain Corbin writes:

The sexologists of the time, and Kraft-Ebing in particular, even propose an explanation: "At a time when dress was establishing a veritable barrier between the sexes, the apron evoked a feminine undergarment and suggested easy intimacy." This fetishism of the apron compelled certain prostitutes to appropriate the attitude of young domestic servants when they worked the streets.[6]

Domestic work was an ideal breeding ground for forms of sexually venal activities; one could imagine a myriad of scenarios, one of which involved a hapless maid yielding to the promises of wealth and security, declarations of love and devotion, by a sexually frustrated bourgeois husband. Given the embourgeoisement of the household, the sexual decorum, and the strictures of Parisian society, there would have been scores of sex-starved, financially secure clients roaming the arrondissements of nineteenth-century Paris in search of women for hire, if the maid was unwilling. Efforts to re-create the

atmosphere and elements of the bourgeois home genuinely bene-
fited the sex trade industry. Brothel keepers whose primary clientele
were comprised of bourgeois men furnished their digs on this order
to appease their clients' class and sexual sensibilities. The illusion
of home tempered the *maison de prostitution* reality.[7] It is hence no
small wonder that street prostitutes, the lowest rung in the hierarchization of *filles de noces*, adopted the tools of trade, or attitude and
uniform, of the domestic servant to increase their allure to clients,
and thus, their profitability.

But the apron and its subsequent fetishization appears to be a much
more complex sexual phenomenom than both Corbin and Krafft-
Ebing realize. Although the numbers of shopkeepers involved in
prostitution also increased, there was no accompanying fetishization of their tools of trade, such as hats, gloves, and the like.

In the early nineteenth century the apron, or the *tablier,* was already fetishized in the French scientific and cultural imagination
thanks to Sarah Bartmann, the Hottentot Venus. Georges Cuvier
wrote in glee upon his discovery of the apron: "There is nothing
more famous . . . than the *tablier* of the Hottentots and at the same
time no feature has been the object of so many arguments." The
conflation of the Venus at this juncture with her apron(s) into the
prostitute body as the quintessence of vice, disease, and venality
is equally noteworthy. It is not mere coincidence that "the most
remarkable particularity of her organization,"[8] her sex, would be
named the apron, that she would be caricatured and exhibited in
an apron, and finally, that her sex, the mysterious Hottentot Apron,
would come to signify disease, vice, and prostitution in nineteenth-
century France.[9] The *apron* covers the *apron*, the corrupting and
venal sex, the prostitute's sex, or the sex of one who has prostitute
proclivities as signified by her trade and dress — that is, the maid.

It is also plausible then that when the late-nineteenth-century
bonne fastened the apron around her waist, she was affixing a highly
charged sexual article from another era about her person; her subsequent sexualization, whether or not she was actively involved in

Femme de Caffre (1790). In François Le Vaillant's *Voyage dans l'intérieur de l'Afrique.* Courtesy of the Sterling Memorial Library, Yale University.

the sex trade, constituted a residue of the urges and repressions associated with Bartmannmania.[10]

It would appear that the association of black women with venal sex and the apron struck a chord with Baudelaire, since there is an overlapping in the images of the seminude muse, Femme caffre, clad in an apron; the Hottentot Venus, from Kaffraria, South Africa, who symbolized venal sexuality through her literal participation in sexualizing exhibitions and the posthumous, revelatory discovery of her Hottentot Apron; and *La Belle Dorothée*, the "Cafrine" (Femme caffre?) and prostitute.

That Baudelaire does his part in maintaining the hierarchy and mastery implicit in the Black Venus narrative is clear. Dorothée is indeed venal, and "parfaitement heureuse" (perfectly happy) (119) at that, in this sexualized state of affairs. As in de Pons's *Ourika, l'Africaine,* in which black slave women are depicted as being eager for and anticipating white male sexual advances, Dorothée contentedly accepts her sexploitation in exchange for trinkets, validation, stories of France, and "piastres" (coins) (119).

But unlike de Pons's work, Baudelaire's prose poem is more than a case of waxing rhapsodic on the black female as venal, savage, and exotic; *La Belle Dorothée* invites serious inquiry into questions of identity and the effects of colonialism on the psyche of the colonized. Dorothée's denegated existence and her longing for Frenchness evoke the dilemma confronting the colonized, that nagging Fanonian question: "In reality, who am I?" — that is, the issues of identity and of identification.[11] And her livelihood as a prostitute is bound up with this identity, which continuously denies her Frenchness and, at one time, rendered her a bondwoman. In essence, Dorothée is black; she is a prostitute because she is a "freed" black woman in the colonies; she can never be French because she is black; she was a slave because she is black. Hence she can exist only as either slave or prostitute in the colonies, because she is a black woman.

The prose poem opens with a contrast of light and dark: Dorothée, walking along the deserted sandy beach at daybreak, makes a "striking and dark mark" on the sun's rays of light (117). As she saunters languidly and coquettishly toward her destination, Baudelaire describes this moving tableau of "The Beautiful Dorothy" as "dark," with an enormous "head of blue-black hair." She has "pointed breasts" and a "slim waist" balanced on "wide hips," with a "superb leg" that peeks out periodically as the sea's breeze lifts the folds of her clinging dress (117). Baudelaire's romantic proclivities are evident in the way he fetishizes Dorothée's foot:

And her foot, like those of the marble goddesses that Europe encloses in museums, imprints faithfully its form on the fine sand. Dorothée is so prodigiously coquettish that the pleasure of being admired outweighs the pride of being freed, so that even though she is free, she walks without shoes. (117–118)

The goddess-like foot becomes a synecdoche for Dorothée's goddess-like persona; it serves equally as a signifier of her venality. She is like the European goddess of love, Venus, but in black, a Black Venus, bringing by "bare foot," venal and exotic pleasures to "some young officer, who on far-off shores heard talk of the famous Dorothée from his comrades" (118).

Dorothée is a "freed" black woman. But the beauty of her foot, fetishized by the Frenchmen with whom she shares her amorous celestial talents because of its familiarity, its similiarity to that of white goddesses, brings more satisfaction to this "simple creature" than her freed status (118). As she walks, she smiles a "white smile," "as if she perceived in the distance a mirror reflecting . . . her beauty" (118). That mirror is Europe — specifically, France. The mirror is not merely reflecting, it is validating, reassuring, Dorothée in her approximations of whiteness.

This is the fate suffered by the disalienated. As Fanon writes of the colonized's dependency complex:

I begin to suffer not from not being white but to the degree that the white imposes discrimination on me, makes me a colonized native, robs me of all worth, all individuality, tells me that I am a parasite in the world, that

I must bring myself as quickly as possible into *step* with the white world. (italics mine)[12]

Dorothée's systemic and systematic denegation has reduced her to a state of sheer mimicry, where being freed, wearing shoes, is eschewed for bared feet, which in the colonies are paradoxically a marker of racial/sexual domination — that is, slavery. It is the young French officers, we are to assume, who dangle European cultural standards of beauty like carrots in Dorothée's ravenous face, who affirm her foot as beautiful, European, white. Bereft of worth as she is, she, in simply trying to *be* beautiful, European, signifies blackness, domination, primitivity — barefootedness. This paradox represents the insidious ways in which the colonizers (the officers, France) keep Dorothée in her place as sexually venal and useful, racially subjugated, and economically dependent, for it is literally via that splendid "foot" *à la mode Européenne* that she will "bring herself as quickly as possible into *step* with the white world," that she embarks upon her sexually exploitative journey at daybreak. Circulated like languid brown currency, shuttled from French officer to officer, she is continuously reinscribed into the racial-sexual political economy as dominated.

Dorothée is duped, misled into believing that she can be like the "beautiful ladies of Paris" (119). *Being like* is not quite the same as *being*. Dorothée is black, as Baudelaire consistently reminds the reader: "sparkling and black stain," the "darkness of her skin," "her dark face" (117). And there are certain inescapable facts about her blackness. Although she is free, she did not come into the world as such. Her blackness is the difference. It represents the unbridgeable gap between the colonized and the colonizer, the black and the white, the French and the Cafrines in this Manichaean world. She cannot slough off her epidermal schema through mimicry. She is a slave of imitation, as Christopher Miller notes.[13] But she is just as much, in Fanonian terms, a slave of the ideas that others have of her. And in the most cutting and abject sense, she is a sex slave, a sexual laborer, a prostitute, participating in "the most outrageous form of sexual oppression, [in] which an individual is forced to sell her body on the basis of both sex and race . . . to survive." [14]

Dorothée's existence is not, however, so onerous, according to the Baudelairian script. If it were not for the greedy master who owns her beautiful eleven-year-old sister, thus compelling her to give him her earnings so she might purchase the child's freedom, Dorothée would be happy. Given the difference that blackness makes, one should reserve one's pitying sighs for Dorothée's futile, pathetic imitations of whiteness — the slave's simple attempts at trying to *be* mistress. "Admired and pampered by everyone," living in her little coquettish hut reminiscent of a "perfect boudoir," the rather narcissistic Dorothée is quite at ease in the sex trade.

Prostitution is not sexual oppression; it is not a mere means of subsistence or survival for "freed" colonized women in the Baudelairian imagination. It is an equitable and fulfilling exchange, a means through which Frenchmen can experience the celebrated sexual artistry of Dorothée, while she, with every crack-of-dawn sexual encounter, with every deposit of precious French seminal liquor, siphons off a bit of validation, of whiteness.

6

Desirous and Dangerous Imaginations:
The Black Female Body and the Courtesan
in Zola's *Thérèse Raquin*

At the first kiss, she revealed herself as a courtesan, adept in the arts of love. — Zola, *Thérèse Raquin*

The theme of the courtesan obsessed the [nineteenth-century] imagination. From the girl with the heart of gold to the pure and simple devouress of inheritances, mulâtresses held all the roles of employment. — Hoffman, *Le Nègre romantique*

The nineteenth century in French literary history can truly be heralded as an epoch that brought about the rise of the fallen woman as subject matter in both realist and naturalist novels. Indeed, prostitution profoundly marked Paris of the day, and the prostitute with her "perverse nature" and "infected sex" quickly became the obsession of regulationists, physicians, and, more to the point for our purposes, writers. But what is most fascinating about this era rife with "women for hire" is that the black female was often conflated with the image of this essentially sexualized woman in the French literary and scientific imagination. From Julien-Joseph Virey's *Histoire naturelle du genre humain* to Charles Baudelaire's *La Belle Dorothée*, to Charles Castellans's *La Mulâtresse* and Eugène Sue's *Mystères de Paris*, the sexualization and the venality of the black female body present themselves as areas of pervasive French male intrigue. Sander Gilman notes:

The prostitute is the essential sexualized female in the nineteenth century. . . . The primitive is the black, and the qualities of blackness, or at least of the black female, are those of the prostitute. . . . The late nineteenth-century perception of the prostitute merged with that of the black.[1]

While Gilman's assessment is, in some respects, accurate, it is nevertheless problematic in that it lacks developed analysis. Although black female sexuality represents for the French the iconography of the prostitute, the actual presence of black women in Paris, and their participation in prostitution in the nineteenth century, was relatively small according to the demographics compiled by celebrated nineteenth-century social anthropologist Alexandre Parent-Duchâtelet:

Out of the 12,707 women registered in Paris since April 16, 1816, at which time we did a general census up to April 31, 1831, that is for 15 years:
24 had never been able to indicate in what countries they were born;
31 came from different foreign countries;
451 belonged to foreign regions of Europe;
12,201 were born in our departments.
Among the 31 foreigners in Europe we counted: 18 Americans, 11 Africans, 2 Asians.[2]

Duchâtelet's study accounts for only registered prostitutes, that is, *filles en carte*. Nonetheless, from the data he concludes that out of the 12,707 registered prostitutes in Paris, only 11 were African. Of the 18 Americans, several were from countries with a predominantly black population: Guadeloupe, Saint Domingue, Martinique, and French Guiana.

Further, historian Hans Werner Debrunner writes that "in spite of sayings as to the lewdness of African girls . . . African prostitutes seem to have been rare if there were any at all."[3] And finally, social anthropologist Fernando Henrique's *Prostitution in Europe and the Americas* reveals:

A particular item from *Les Bordels de Paris* is worth quoting. This concerns a brothel of Negro women. For those who wished to indulge their taste for the exotic there was a brothel of Negro women at the house of Mademoiselle Isabeau, formerly at the rue Neuve de Montmorency but now at the house of M. Marchand, pawnbroker in rue Xaintoge. There is no fixed price. Negro women, mustees (lightly coloured), mulattoes are sold, as women are sold from an oriental caravan. The existence of such a brothel seems to show that coloured women were in demand as prostitutes. This can be taken as an indication of a genuine liking for such whores, or their scarcity value in the Paris of the day.[4]

Despite contrary factual evidence, it is clear that the presence of black women in significant numbers working as "filles de noces" (women for hire) was not a prerequisite for the French writer to imagine the black woman as a prostitute. One black prostitute or eleven African prostitutes represents all those absent black women as prostitutes, and overshadows, indeed erases, the presence of over twelve thousand white prostitutes. In essence, one African prostitute represents over one thousand white prostitutes. Even if one classifies all 18 "American" prostitutes as black (which the social anthropologist does not), bringing the sum total of black women involved in the Parisian sex trade industry in the mid–nineteenth century to 29, 1 black prostitute would represent 437 white ones. Yet the psychosexual/racial dilemma implicit in this iconographization remains unresolved. Indeed, Henrique's observation that "coloured women were in demand as prostitutes" and that this "can be taken as an indication of a genuine liking for such whores" is at the root of the polemic and offers a point of entry for our discussion.

The French Male Psyche in Question:
Reckless Desires and Dangerous Imaginations

The collapse of the black female body into that of the prostitute body appears essentially attributable to the conflicting impulses of repulsion/repression and attraction operating within the French male psyche. Indeed, at the root of such a construction is desire—a conquering desire to know, on the one hand, and to master through representation, on the other. Scopophilia is the erotic investment of the desire to know in a body of difference. The body toward which this desire has been directed is profoundly different, racially and sexually. But what is so different from the self is necessarily feared and forbidden; this difference and its subsequent prohibition and inaccessibility make the object of the look all the more desirable to know, to conquer. A certain conflict occurs in the male psyche between the desire to know that strange body and a social morality that restricts the male's sexual gratification and affirms an imposed sexual and racial order.[5] This crisis requires a divestment of pleasurable desire and an investment of negativity, a projection of the undesirable onto the desired, yet feared object. The gaze is thwarted, since it cannot decipher or pleasurably contemplate black femininity, since it evokes fear/guilt because of its quintessential difference. What the gaze cannot discern, from a safer distance, it constructs. Black women thus came to represent that which the European male could not articulate without psychic crises: uninhibited sexuality. And uninhibited sexuality is presumably a characteristic of the prostitute.

The Prostitute Body in Question

"Prostitution, in the nineteenth century, is an indispensable excremental phenomenon that protects the social body...."[6] Accordingly, the prostitute is an undesirable, but simultaneously desired body, a polluting, necessary evil. Due to demographic changes, the shortage of women, and the embourgeoisement of society, which led to sexual privation and the respectable bourgeois mother-woman, the demand for venal sex in the nineteenth century greatly increased.[7] This repressive sexual morality and the romantic idealization of the bourgeois woman made wives, "respectable" single young women, and pubescent girls sexually inaccessible. The prostitute was paid to do what these respectable women could not: give and perhaps receive uninhibited pleasures — for money. The prostitute was paid to take a loss in her social standing.

The body of the prostitute is an indecipherable terrain of contestation. She becomes in the nineteenth century an object of inquiry as to the workings of her sex, her psychology, her physiology:

5. *Some words about the state within which are found the prostitute's sexual parts.* If there is an opinion generally admitted and not yet contradicted, it is that the genitalia of prostitutes *must* show some adaptation and particular character, as an inevitable consequence of their trade. . . . The genitalia of prostitutes do not demonstrate any special adaptation that is particular to them; in this respect, there is no difference between those of prostitutes and those of the most faithful married women.[8]

6. *What is the primary cause of prostitution?* We must constantly keep in mind that the girls who devote themselves to public prostitution have already lived during a time more or less long in disorder.[9]

1. *Peculiar plumpness of many prostitutes.* The plumpness of many prostitutes, and their brilliant state of health, strikes everyone who sees them. . . . It is necessary to attribute the often remarkable plumpness of prostitutes to the large number of hot baths that they take for the most part, and above all to the inactive life that the majority of them lead, and to the abundance of food that they eat. Indifferent to the future, eating at every instance, consuming much more than other hardworking working-class women, rising at ten or eleven o'clock each morning, how with such an animal-like life, would they not fatten themselves up?[10]

The prostitute's genitalia are no different from those of the faithfully married woman. This indistinguishability requires that the activities of women in general, and prostitutes specifically, be closely monitored. The prostitute's body is characterized by its plumpness, the result of her delight in food, inactive trade that requires that she do nothing more than lie on her back, and constant baths. She is a *mangeuse*, greedily and lazily feasting off life itself. She represents female disorder and excess, woman's sex and mouth out of control, on the margins of patriarchal order. In the recesses of Parent-Duchâtelet's study, uncertainty lurks. He cannot paint, even with the help of the sciences of phrenology, physiognomy, and physiology, a prototype of a prostitute.

The physical diversity among prostitutes—specifically, unregistered sex workers—makes them supremely dangerous. Because of, according to Parent-Duchâtelet, the temporary nature of the profession, the unregistered fille can reenter society and cause disorder and disruption by producing pathological offspring. The prostitute's body and its potential mobility represent a source of class confusion, a threat to the meticulously class-delineated social order. And thus, she must be carefully scrutinized and regulated. She remains incomprehensible and undetectable to the savant's gaze. And this indecipherability resulted in a myriad of deductions as to her participation in prostitution.

And while Parent-Duchâtelet's study suggests that economic hardship stemming from promises of marriage followed by abandonment by lovers, impregnation by employers rapidly succeeded by termination of employment, or coercion by a lover often leads to prostitution,[11] two ideas associated with the prostitute dominate the nineteenth century: insatiability and genealogy. The latter motif is clearly presented in Emile Zola's chefs d'oeuvre, *Nana* and *Thérèse Raquin*.

Emile Zola's *Mariage d'amour*

The idea that sexual disorder is hereditary resonates throughout Zola's writing on the prostitute. If *Nana* is destined for a life of debauchery and vice because of her degenerate alcoholic family, then Thérèse, the quintessential *mulâtresse* stereotype, who commits adultery and murder and then falls into the demimonde of Paris, is overcome by the "immorality and lascivious sensuality of the blacks that flowed within her veins."[12] The mulâtresse is an obsession of the nineteenth-century literary imagination. This mixed-race female personage is always endowed with a physical whiteness that ob-scures her "dangerous" blackness. Blood is fetishized in Zola's novel-las. And true to the literary creed of naturalism, black blood or *sang africain* has far-reaching, hereditary implications in *Thérèse Raquin*.

Thérèse Raquin first appeared in *Le Figaro* on December 24, 1866, under the title *Un Mariage d'amour*. The novel was published again as *Un Mariage d'amour* in three parts in the August, September, and October 1867 issues of *L'Artiste*. Finally, in December 1867, Zola published the work as a whole under the title *Thérèse Raquin*.

Provoking outrage and scandal, the novel was immediately labeled as a premier example of *la littérature putride,* and literary critic Louis Ulbach Ferragus accused Zola of being "a miserable hysteric who entertains himself by writing pornography":[13]

Established since a number of years is a monstrous school of novelists.... It is easier to write a brutal novel, full of purulence, crime and prostitu-tion, than to write a contained, measured, subtle novel, pointing out in-famies, without exposing them, rousing without disgust.... My curiosity has recently slipped in a puddle of filth and blood which calls itself *Thérèse Raquin,* whose author, Mr. Zola, passes for a young man of talent.[14]

Filth, blood, crime, and prostitution are the sum total of *Thérèse Raquin,* according to Ferragus, and Emile Zola, that monstrous natu-ralist, masquerades as a talented writer. Zola responded to Ferragus's abrasive critique eight days later in a letter to *Le Figaro*.[15] And in April 1868, the second edition of the book was published with an added preface by Zola in which he attempted to explain his inten-tions in creating the book as well as the literary creed of naturalism: "In *Thérèse Raquin,* I wanted to study temperaments. . . . This is the entire point of the book. I chose characters dominated com-pletely by their nerves and blood, deprived of free will, led to each act of their life by the fatalities of their flesh" (59–60). Naturalism takes as its point of departure physiology and physiognomy. Like a surgeon with a cadaver, Zola dissects and reads bodies in order to reveal propensities. Certainly, as Zola maintains, *Thérèse Raquin* is a study of temperaments. However, the novel goes beyond this simple study, particularly in light of the revisions Zola made to the original manuscript, *Un Mariage d'amour*.[16] While the plots of *Un Mariage d'amour* and *Thérèse Raquin* are virtually the same—both involving adultery, murder, remorse, and suicide—the names of the characters are different: originally they were named Suzanne, Michel, and Jacques. The first publication of this novella in 1866 did not mention the explicit courtesanlike nature of Suzanne. By the final drafts and publication, Zola had not only added the themes of prostitution and induced abortion, but he had also changed the title and the names of the main characters—who were now Camille, Laurent, and Thérèse—and racialized the female protagonist.

Throughout all three versions of the narrative, Zola insists upon the "nervosité naturelle" (natural excitation) of the female protagonist. After publishing excerpts with a white heroine, Zola, in the final publication, darkens the heroine, as if the pathological behavior is more characteristic of the mulâtresse, because of her African origins. Unlike Nana, whose devouring sexuality is attributed to her degenerate working-class origins and feeds upon Parisian society's upper crust, Thérèse, a woman raised in the comforts and confines of the bourgeoisie, has an ardent sexuality that is attributed to her lower racial origins and that finds gratification among the lower classes (that is, with Laurent and prostitutes).[17] Suzanne, ironically, finds her way back into the novel, but as the bourgeois, asexual wife of Olivier.

The Painterly Text:
Olympia and Thérèse, the Prostitute and the Mulâtresse

Another revealing aspect of the novel is the similarity between Zola's study of Edouard Manet's *Olympia* and his portraiture of Thérèse. During the writing of *Thérèse Raquin*, Zola frequented the painter's studio. *Thérèse Raquin* has been called a painterly text by some literary critics.[18] An avid admirer of Manet's work, Zola heralded *Olympia* as the painter's chef d'oeuvre. A scandal in nineteenth-century

Paris, and thus excluded from the Exposition Universelle of 1867, *Olympia* features a nude prostitute with her black female servant and a cat: venal female sexuality in all of its debased resplendence. The muse's hand carefully conceals her genitals. The famous pussy (cat) not only symbolizes her hidden genitals, but the prostitute's animality.[19] The black female servant, as Sander Gilman has noted, represents the primitive sexual nature of the fille.[20]

Reviewing the work in *Revue du dix-neuvième siècle,* Zola applauds Manet for translating the essence of all the "créatures" in the painting:

Olympia, laid upon white sheets, makes a large pale stain upon the black background: within this dark background is the head of the black woman . . . and that famous cat. . . . Look at the face of the young girl: the lips are two thin rose lines, the eyes reduce themselves to dark strokes. . . . When our artists give us Venuses, they correct nature, they lie. Edouard Manet asked himself why lie, why not speak the truth; he introduced us to Olympia, this prostitute of our day, whom you meet on the sidewalks. . . . You [Manet] have admirably succeeded . . . in translating energetically and within a special language the truths of light and darkness, the realities of all the objects and creatures.[21]

Eleven months after Zola's review, Olympia's "deux minces lignes roses" (two thin rose lines) and "les yeux se réduisent à quelque traits noirs" (the eyes reduce themselves to dark strokes) figured in *Thérèse Raquin,* although slightly changed "deux minces traits d'un rose pâle" (two thin strokes of a pale rose) and as "l'œil noir" (dark eye) (67). *Olympia,* the painting and the fille, represents a contrast between light and darkness, black and white. For all her apparent whiteness, the fille is deftly dark, staining, even in her paleness, the dark background. Within Thérèse's body, Zola has fused the light and darkness, the "realities," of all three of the painting's creatures — a white body (Olympia) governed by "the lascivious sensuality of the blacks that flows in its veins" (the black female servant) and animality (the famous cat). The character Thérèse also owns a complicitous and duplicitous cat, which is strangled by Laurent.

Thérèse Raquin exists as more than the study of temperaments; it is, more specifically, a study of the temperament and proclivities of a body dictated by the conflictual intersection of race, sexuality, class, and gender, that is, the sexualized, *embourgeoised* black female body.

The novella opens with a description of the humid, gloomy passage of the Pont Neuf. This passage leads to the equally musty and humid boutique called *Thérèse Raquin*. Through the window of the boutique emerges "a pale and grave profile of a young woman" (67). The profile belongs to Thérèse. Zola continues his description of the young woman:

This profile emerged vaguely from the shadows that reigned within the boutique. . . . a long, narrow, keen nose; the lips were two thin strokes of a pale pink, and the chin, small and firm, was attached to the neck by a fleshy and supple jawline. One could not see the body, which was lost in the shadow; the profile alone appeared, and from a flat whiteness, peered a widely opened dark eye, as if it were crushed under a mass of dark hair. (65)

Much like the muse of Manet's *Olympia*, Thérèse is presented as a white mark on a dark background. Pale, thin-lipped, and keen-nosed, Thérèse is physiognomically European. Her body, however, is enveloped in shadows. A fusion of black and white, her excessive nature is intimated by Zola's use of sexualized adjectives—"supple and fleshy"—to describe her jawline. While the female body is generally constructed as an enigmatic, dark terrain, Thérèse's bodily opacity relates particularly to her mysterious, African origins.

She is the offspring of "a daughter of a tribal chief in Africa" (94) and a Frenchman, Captain Degans. Arriving from Algeria sixteen years earlier, Degans left the infant Thérèse with his sister, Madame Raquin, who is a haberdasher. Knowing very little about her niece's origins except that she was born in Oran and that her mother was an indigenous woman of great beauty, the haberdasher adopts and raises the child in bourgeois comforts.

Zola blends orientalism and africanism in this novella. However,

africanism seems to move to the fore as he falls back on the Black
Venus narrative. Although Thérèse was born in Algeria, Zola elimi-
nates all Arab/North African and racial/cultural specificity by refer-
ring to her as simply African later in the text. Thérèse is half African;
thus, for Zola, she is pure, uncompromisingly black. Africa is perceived as dark, black. Blackness signifies, among other things, perverse sexuality and animality. As such, Zola proceeds by contrasting
Thérèse's pale, calm, indifferent exterior with her repressed ardent,
high-strung interior. Her embourgeoisement has caused her to de-
velop a placid exterior in order to hide "the passions of her nature":

This life of forced convalescence turned her in upon herself; she acquired
the habit of speaking in a whisper, of walking without making a sound,
of remaining quiet and motionless. . . . But when she raised an arm, or
put a foot forward, one sensed her feline suppleness, strong and powerful
muscles, stored energy, a passion that slept within her dormant flesh.[22] . . .
Her aunt had repeated so often, "Be quiet," that she possessed a supreme
coolness, a seeming tranquillity that hid terrible fits of passion. (72)

Plagued by fits of passion, Thérèse creates an emotionless mask to
conceal her ardent nature. This deliberate repression is nonetheless
betrayed by her simplest gestures. Thérèse is sex in motion, a passionate and exotic feline, alienated from her cloistering milieu. Her
adaptation to the "habits of the bourgeois family" (80) renders her
"a passive instrument" (79).

Upon reaching her twenty-first birthday, Thérèse marries her
sickly cousin, Camille. Eight days after the marriage, the couple and
Madame Raquin move to Paris. This rather schematic geographic
move, the exodus from Vernon (the quaint countryside) to Paris (the
bustling, prostitute-ridden city), symbolizes a shift from bourgeois
goodness to vice, from the repression of black female sexuality to
its dangerous unleashing. For it is in Paris that Thérèse meets Laurent, her lover, accomplice in the drowning of Camille, and second
husband.

She is fascinated by the aspiring painter:

She had never seen a real man. Laurent, tall, strong, fresh-faced, astonished her. She contemplated with a sort of admiration his low forehead . . . his full cheeks, his red lips, his regular face, of a full-blooded beauty. She momentarily fixed her gaze upon his neck; this neck was broad and short, thick and powerful. . . . Laurent was truly a peasant's son. . . . One sensed that underneath his clothes were hard and developed muscles, an entire body of solid and firm flesh. . . . And Thérèse examined him with curiosity, going from his fists to his face, experiencing little thrills when her eyes rested upon his bull-like neck. (84)

Laurent is the symbol of machismo and virility in all of its peasant vulgarity. Zola, in his description of Laurent, seems bent on appealing to nineteenth-century class stereotypes. Laurent's brutish physiognomy and physiology are a result of his peasant background. From his low forehead to his red lips, thick, bull-like neck, and firm flesh, his body oozes primitiveness and hot-bloodedness. Pseudoscience and cultural/class stereotypes are fused and reinforce one another. Laurent's low forehead is a sign of irreflection, irrationality, and impulsiveness.[23] He is all body, no head, lacking in reason, driven purely by emotion.

The grossness that Zola uses to describe Laurent corresponds to this character's general disposition and motivation for embarking upon an affair with Thérèse — laziness and greed:

He was a sluggard, having corpulent appetites, desires satiated by easy and lasting pleasures. This large, powerful body asked only to do nothing, except to wallow endlessly in idleness and self-indulgence. . . . He had thrown himself into art, hoping to find a trade for the lazy. (85)

Laurent has an unquenchable appetite for food, women, money, and other earthly pleasures; he is a gourmand, consuming and draining pleasurable resources. He desires to immerse himself in inactive life.

Linked like kindred spirits, the bull and the feline, the peasant and the masquerading bourgeois woman, Laurent and Thérèse are "brutes humaines." [24] Thérèse and Laurent emblematize the primitive, the sexual, the coming together of the lower class and sex and race. These two disorderly, dangerous bodies (the one a product of miscegenation cloaked in whiteness, thus carrying the disease of perverse sexuality; the other, a vulgar peasant attempting to transcend class boundaries), disastrously fated, destroy the monotony of bourgeois order.

The tension between Thérèse and Laurent mounts and results in savagely, gratifying adulterous sex. Thérèse is completely transformed from an "unsatiated woman" into "a strange beauty." The pleasurable exploration of her sexuality has literally metamorphosed her placid, tranquil exterior. The exploration of female sexuality opens up a discourse loaded with racial/sexual stereotypes on the inherent nature of black femaleness:

At the first kiss, she revealed herself as a courtesan, adept in the arts of love. Her unsatiated body threw itself madly into sensual pleasure; she awakened as if from a dream, she was born to passion. . . . All the instincts of this high-strung woman burst with an unprecedented violence; the blood of her mother, that African blood which was burning within her veins, began to flow, to beat furiously within her frail body. . . . She exposed herself, she offered herself with a supreme immodesty. (93)

A true Venus, Thérèse need not practice her arts; they come naturally. Having never experienced sexual fulfillment, she instinctively knows how to give and receive unrestrained pleasures. Her courtesan nature is unveiled with one kiss. Passion is Thérèse's birthright, an inheritance from her *sang africain*. Her mother's blood, burning in her veins but hitherto constantly repressed, bursts through with effervescence. Unleashed at last, the African blood—that spring of sexuality made up of plasma and sensual, passionate blood cells—pumps life into Thérèse's frail body.

Not only is Thérèse's body liberated, but so is her voice. After years of virtual silence and enclosure within herself, she boasts of her African ancestry, comparing it with the inhibiting, convalescent existence that she has been forced to live:

But I would have preferred abandonment to their hospitality. . . . They told me that my mother was the daughter of a tribal chief in Africa; I often thought of her and I realized that I belonged to her by blood and instincts. . . . they have buried me alive in this ignoble boutique. . . . They have turned me into a hypocrite and a liar. . . . They have suffocated me within their bourgeois refinements. (94–95)

Thérèse masquerades as a respectable woman. This bourgeois charade has virtually suffocated her, choked the vitality out of her. The awakening of black blood leads Thérèse to commit transgressions that are uncharacteristic of the nineteenth-century bourgeois woman: murder, abortion, and, finally, prostitution. She reveals herself as a courtesan and Laurent calls her a *prostituée* (223), for it is her corrupting sex that seduced him to murder Camille. The essential difference between the courtesan and the bourgeois woman is "pudeur" (modesty). According to Parent-Duchâtelet, modesty is the most precious attribute of femininity.[25] Thérèse lacks pudeur. Indeed, she offers herself with a supreme "impudeur."

Thérèse naturally seeks refuge in the demimonde to escape Laurent and the ominous memory of the drowned Camille:

He saw Thérèse quickly leave the passage . . . and for the first time, he noticed that she was dressed like a prostitute, in a dress with a long train; she was swaying on the sidewalk in a provocative fashion, looking at men, raising the front of her skirt very high. . . . Thérèse was making her way toward a cafe. . . . She sat down in the middle of a group of women and students, at one of the tables set on the sidewalk. She gave familiar handshakes to everyone. . . . She seemed at home, she was talking with a fair young man. . . . Two prostitutes came bending over the table that she occupied, addressing her familiarly in their hoarse voices. . . . Around her, women were smoking, the men were openly kissing the women. . . . When Thérèse had finished her absinthe, she stood up, took the arm of the fair young man and descended the street. . . . he believed he saw the fair young man's hands sliding around Thérèse's waist. (242–43)

After living a life of hypocrisy masquerading as a bourgeois woman, Thérèse finds her niche among Paris's *filles de noce*. Rather than being ill at ease, she is at home, familiarly giving handshakes and addressed by the hoarse-voiced filles, who use the familiar "*tu*." Swaying provocatively down the street, she allows her immodest nature to take its course. Beginning with her adulterous tryst with Laurent, Thérèse's gradual *chute* from respectability to the demimonde is a result of her pathological genealogy, her Africanness. Linking discourses on race, gender, class mobility, and sexuality, Zola fashions *Thérèse Raquin* into a novel representing the intersection of two feared, desired bodies of the nineteenth-century literary and social imagination: the black female body and the prostitute body.

7

Can a White Man Love a Black Woman?

Perversions of Love beyond the Pale in

Maupassant's "Boitelle"

Today I believe in the possibility of love; that is why I endeavor to trace its imperfections, its perversions. — Frantz Fanon, *Black Skin, White Masks*

Interracial sex — specifically, sex between French men and African and Antillean women — is a well-noted phenomenon in the history of the more personal relations between whites and blacks. But love presents itself as an altogether slippery emotion, which seems somehow to elude these relations historically premised upon coercion and power, or hampered by, in the words of Fanon, "that feeling of inferiority or that Adlerian exaltation, that overcompensation, which seem to be the indices of the black *Weltanschauung*."[1] Fanon investigated the possibility of authentic interracial love for an Antillean female psyche at odds with itself, but our angle is wholly different. If the feeling of inferiority often pervades the black female psyche, whisking her into the arms of a white knight who alone can endow her existence with value, and thus inadvertently inhibiting authentic love, can the white male psyche escape the feeling of superiority, his birthright as purveyor of value, and transcend the temptation of self-praise for his openness to difference, and really love a black woman?

White supremacy takes many forms, from extreme hatred of difference to an intensified adoration of *Other* bodies. The exoticist represents the latter supremacist. He contemplates black women as mere objects, things to be possessed, in his world of collectible exotica. In the exoticist's world, the black female provides rapturous delights, a detour from the ennui of whiteness. Black women serve as savorous spices, seasonings that come in a variety of colors and ethnic flavors to whet the exoticist's palate. Exoticism is thus a perversion of love.

We find this perversion neatly presented under the guise of progressivism in naturalist writer Guy de Maupassant's eight-page short story, "Boitelle" (1889),[2] which takes as its subject matter unrequited "love" and racial prejudice.

The tale is set between the country village of Tourteville and the bustling port city of Le Havre, and our protagonist, Antoine Boitelle, is a simple Normand peasant and father of fourteen children. Boitelle, a worker specializing in dirty jobs involving sewage and cesspools, plies his trade with indifference and resignation. We are told that he is thoroughly lacking in ambition, and that his indifference and undesirable occupational choice are linked to the feelings of loss and denial imposed on him by his parents some years before. When asked about his adult children's spousal choices, Boitelle cautions:

I didn't oppose them. I didn't oppose them in anything. They married as they wanted. It is important not to oppose tastes — it turns out badly. If I am a sewage worker — well, it is because my parents opposed my tastes. If not, I would have become a worker like the others. [2: 1086]

Those opposed tastes were for things exotic, specifically a black woman.

The young Antoine Boitelle was a military officer stationed in Le Havre. During his leisure he would visit the merchants on the quay who sold birds from all over the world:

He would go on his way slowly along the cages with the parrots with green backs and yellow heads from the Amazon, the parrots with gray backs and red heads from Senegal, the enormous macaws . . . the little jumping birds, red, yellow, blue . . . from a faraway and mystical forest. . . . Looking at the monkeys also gave him great pleasure, and he could not imagine a grander luxury for a wealthy man than to possess these animals as one has dogs and cats. [2:1087]

Passively gazing outward, Boitelle contemplates and seizes all the exotic fauna in his sight. He wants to possess these wild animals from distant, mysterious forests like domesticated pets. The "taste for the exotic is in [his] blood" (2:1087).

One day, in an ecstatic moment of contemplating a "monstrous" macaw from South America, Boitelle fixates on a young Negress: "The attention of Boitelle was equally shared between the animal and the woman, and he could not have said really which one of these two beings he was contemplating with the most astonishment and pleasure" (2:1087). The white male gaze is suspended between the black woman and the animal. Boitelle's tropical landscape offers a menu of wild birds, monkeys, and a black woman. And our viewer cannot decide which to devour, from which object he derives the most pleasure in looking; he is caught between the magnificent plumes of the South American bird and the colorfully attired young Negress.

In one fell swoop, Boitelle objectifies and reduces the black woman not only to a quasi-bountiful rarity to be tasted and sampled, but also to a state of animality through the comparative gaze. The Negress's animality is again presented one page later when Maupassant refers to her as "this little black animal" (2:1088). Besides the immediate stereotyped connotations of the comparison — woman=animal, black=animal=sexual savagery — the significance of this configuration will be particularly telling by the conclusion of the story.

Boitelle appreciates racial-sexual difference through exoticism. It is this taste for difference, the desire to possess and experience blackness and thus flee banality, that leads him to "cherish" the nameless Negress.[3] The fact that she has no name, no identity, further points to her objectified positionality. She is simply referred to as "the negress," or the property of the white male: "his negress," "my negress."

As much as Boitelle might be seduced by difference, he nevertheless reigns it into the familiar space of sameness: "One day finally, he was very surprised in confirming that she spoke French like everyone" (2:1088). With each encounter, the Negress's difference manifests itself "as almost the same but not quite":[4] "The ideas of this negress were the same as the practical ideas of the young women of the country—she respected practicality, work, religion, good conduct . . ." (2:1088). The Negress is like all the practical young women of Normandy, but she is, at least for the exoticist's purposes, black—different. Difference is put to use to reinscribe the status quo, that is, white ideas and cultural values. Boitelle can enjoy his "taste for the exotic," can transcend the mundanity of day-to-day white existence, through his exploitation of this nameless Negress without ever subverting a Eurocentered hierarchy of values.

Same-difference manifests itself on another level with the Negress. She is not African, but she is not European. She is, we are to assume, from the newly conquered world of America: "She was dropped off on the quay of Havre by an American captain. This captain had found her when she was about six years old . . . some hours after his departure from New York" (2:1088). The Negress is from that remote continent explored by French travelers and rhapsodized over at length by romantic writers such as Chateaubriand. She is American—but here again, familiarity is invoked. Despite its geographic remoteness, its cultural newness, America is wholly familiar; it is part of the Occident.

Antoine wants to marry this wonder of a woman. However, he must convince his parents that the Negress is worthy of his gift of love. Taking her to Tourteville, he beams with pride at the attention she garners (2:1090). She is a spectacle, eliciting fear (screams from children) and wondrous desire (curious stares from adults). Locked arm-in-arm with the Negress, the exoticist basks in the wonder that blackness commands. She is, after all, "his negress" (2:1094). She is worn like a rare badge, a testament to Boitelle's difference, his transcendence.

Much to the young peasant's chagrin, the Negress is "too black" to be loved (2:1092), too different for the Boitelles, in spite of her sameness. No matter what she does to prove her worthiness—cooking, cleaning, laughing on cue—the yardstick of whiteness is cast out and she falls dismally short. Indeed, she is frightening to these eyes that have never conceptualized humanity in a black face (2:1090). Her very presence turns their blood, paralyzes their emotions, and conjures up images of the devil (2:1091–92). Blackness is abject, evil, and dirty—for example, the mother inquires, "It [blackness] does not soil the sheets?" (2:1090).

Dumbfounded and crushed, Boitelle must give up his Negress, or at least what she represents, and recreate a semblance of difference in the banal space of Tourteville's sameness—hence his lack of ambition and his odorous livelihood. The filth of his trade replaces the "soil" signified by the Negress.

As for his wife, Boitelle declares, "She has not displeased me, since I have fourteen children" (2:1094). But when asked about the Negress, he proffers: " '*My negress,*' she had only to look at me and I felt like I was transported" (2:1094; italics mine). What value does the simple look from the "too black," nameless female object have for the white male? And does Boitelle love this black woman? The "look" betrays the farce, the possibility of "love." The love of the Negress is indeed the love of the self (love is fundamentally narcissistic, according to Jean-Paul Sartre and Jacques Lacan, among others). The Negress affirms Boitelle's being as purveyor of value; she functions as a reflective instrument, as marginalized eyes that stare back without judgment, as one forever grateful for his love no matter how self-interested and perverse, like an exotic macaw.

There is no love here; there are merely perversions of love. As Frantz Fanon admonishes, "The man who *loves* the Negro is as sick as the one who abominates him." [5]

8

Bamboulas, Bacchanals, and Dark Veils over

White Memories in Loti's *Le Roman d'un spahi*

In the March–May 1881 issues of *La Nouvelle Revue,* the editor, Mme. Juliette Adams, published the sentimental adventures of a French cavalryman in West Africa. The title of the serialized novel was *Le Spahi.* Its author, Louis Marie Julien Viaud, popularly known as Pierre Loti, was considered a connoisseur of the bizarre, a chronicler of difference whose masterful *récits* thrived upon the idea of the Other as savage and primitive. If ever there was a nineteenth-century novelist whose writerly endeavors made the strange familiar to French audiences, who wholly exemplified the colonialist mentality of his era, it was Pierre Loti.

Unlike many of his predecessors in the genre of travel novels, Loti's mythic narratives had the stamp of authenticity. While Diderot's "imagination traveled for him" in his exoticizing tract on Tahitian sexuality, *Le Supplément au voyage de Bougainville,* Loti was a sailor whose maritime career took him to the ports of Tahiti, Japan, Turkey, Senegal, and various other "exotic" locales.

Besides providing ethnographic snapshots of flora and fauna, Loti peoples his primitive landscapes with exotic and lusty women. Loti's orientalist novels (as this genre of writing about far-flung lands and slavish, wayward women has been dubbed) follow a narrative pattern in which an exotic female savage becomes pivotal, indeed essential, to the *œuvres'* flow: the hero arrives, becomes sexually entangled with a native woman, verbally and mentally abuses the white male–

worshiping native, and departs, leaving the woman heartbroken and wholly degraded, or dead.[1]

Although *Le Roman d'un spahi* appears to follow this pattern, its plot structure veers from the standard Loti fare of exotica and sexual conquest. Notwithstanding its orientalist allusions, Arabs, harems, veils, and fezzes, *Le Roman d'un spahi* is an Africanist work. As in Baudelaire's *La Belle Dorothée,* black is the difference. The specifically black African location in which the novel's events take place, the death of the hero, heroine, and their progeny, and the fitting (at least in the narrator's/Loti's eyes) brutal *physical* abuse of the heroine—all these represent a shift from the orientalist works and converge into a particular commentary on race mixing, on the utter and unmendable differences that blackness makes, differences that Loti painstakingly aims to emphasize as "nigger" (nègres) differences.[2]

But more important to this rereading of *Le Roman d'un spahi* in its more appropriate context of French Africanism is Loti's deployment of the Black Venus narrative centered around the bodies and sexualities of two female protagonists: a mulatto woman, Cora, and an African, Fatou-gaye.[3]

Through his depiction of these two bewitching and cuckolding heroines, Loti again attempts to invoke racial difference with sexualized and sexualizing (for black females) implications. Both women are characterized as "keepers of the impalpable gate that opens into a realm of orgies,"[4] as high priestesses of sexual delirium, as black bacchantes. Despite Cora's near-perfect whiteness, her resemblance in dress and manners to an elegant Parisian, she cannot slough off her penchant for multiple sexual partners, bestiality, and sexual degradation in a classic "whore/madonna" complex. Possessing a genealogical defect—her status as a "petite fille d'une esclave"—she cannot resist "falling back into the pit of niggerhood."[5] And for Fatou-gaye, the "little creature" (61) who sleeps at the hero's feet, who is trapped in her corporeality—hence by every imaginable Lotian idea of blackness, of Africanness—life is one frenzied orgiastic *bamboula* after another. Beckoned by the mating call of spring, "Anamalis fobil" (111), a Lotian Africanist neologism, blaring from the griots' tom-toms, Fatou-gaye dutifully responds. It is at these "terribly licentious" (150) primal lovefests that the barely nubile African perfects her "nigger love" (amour nègre) (111), which later seduces and ravages the spahi's "dignité d'*homme blanc*" (*white man*'s dignity; Loti's emphasis) (180).

This strange land of Senegal is presented by Loti as a land of death. A predecessor to that annoying sun in Camus' *L'Etranger,* the sun of Saint Louis is unbearable, torrid, and a constant source of Jean Peyral's ennui, a reminder of his exilic existence. In the course of his ethnographic pursuits, Loti seems almost obsessional in his desire to describe the African landscape and the "heat" of the sun (1). The devouring sun represents the first marker of this land's difference from France. As Léon Fanoudh-Seifer notes, "The word 'sun' reappears 78 times in Loti's text. . . . The frequency of the word is significant: it fixes the myth of the burning country."[6] The hotness of the sun inevitably translates into the hotness of the country and its women. Senegal, its women, and indeed the continent of Africa will be more specifically fixed as not only a source of hotness, of unbearable heat, but as always in heat.

Our first native encounter in the burning country is with "gorilla-faced" men who possess a noteworthy "nigger perseverance" (3). The faraway land's inhabitants are of such a degree of blackness that they immediately conjure up bestial images. Just how their peculiar genre of perseverance is exhibited is never explored; it is a matter of their *being;* it just *is.* Throughout the novel, *nègre* or *noir* is used as an adjective—as a descriptor of difference. Simple functions translate into marked black or nigger difference: "nigger city" (76); "nigger sweat" (76); "nigger politics" (225); "in the niggardly manner," as in comportment (156); "black lips" (35); "black prayer" (200). Dissimilarity is found everywhere in this black country with its black inhabitants. Yet it is a difference that is significantly inferior and wholly impure. Africa is that cursed "land of Cain" (110).

Out of all this steamy hotness and blackness emerges a handsome spahi, Jean Peyral. As an import from the picturesque village of Cevennes in France, Jean Peyral's "pure white[ness]" (8), and we are assured of his purity by Loti, has already been soiled. Handsome though he is, his face and chest have been heavily bronzed by the African sun (8). Suffering from intense melancholia and feelings of profound exile, doing battle with his sensuality in a land where one wallows in lust, the spahi has left in France a devoted cousin/fiancée, Jeanne Méry, as well as an adoring mother and father who greatly depend for their well-being on his generous monthly allotment. At the same time, their letters to the spahi act as his moral conscience, inciting frequent *crises de conscience*.

However, the reader immediately learns that the spahi has been remiss in his monthly duties, that his whiteness has been horribly tainted, that the hard-earned *khâliss* destined for his parents have been spent to purchase silver bracelets for a bamboula, that he has been sexually bewitched and stripped of white dignity by his African mistress, Fatou-gaye:

[Fatou-gaye] knew what catlike caresses to bestow upon her lover; she knew how to put around him her dark arms encircled in silver, beautiful as the arms of a statue; how to rest her nude bosom on the red woolen vest in order to excite those feverish desires that would lead to a pardon for her wrong. . . . And the spahi allowed himself to nonchalantly fall upon his bed near her, putting off until the next day the search for the money that one awaits over there, in the thatched cottage of his elderly parents. (21–22)

But Fatou-gaye is not the first black woman to cause Peyral to lose his head. In fact, we are told that Fatou-gaye was a mere adolescent, walking around practically nude and with an unusual hairstyle, when she first encountered the spahi. She was a Khasson who was captured by the Moors and sold into slavery to a mulattress, Cora, who was the spahi's first lover. It was Fatou-gaye who would save Peyral from the deathly love sickness brought on by the unpitying Cora.

Struggling to avoid the bordellos with their "ignoble mulatto prostitution" and extravagant bacchanals encouraged by absinthe and the climate of Africa, the handsome Peyral is naturally spotted first by the mulattress in the streets:

A woman was especially looking at Jean, a woman who was more elegant and prettier than the others. It was a mulattress, someone was saying, but so white, so white, that someone said a Parisian. . . . [she was] white and pale, of a Spanish pallor, with reddish blond hair—the blond of mulattos—and large round eyes of blue . . . as she was enveloping him in her gaze, he experienced a sort of shiver. (40–41)

Loti plays upon the myth of the idyllic beauty of mulattresses. Cora is not just white, but *so* white that her admixture is perceived only through her "mulatto" blond hair and eyes, which evoke a "Creole languor" (40). Repulsed by the African women, Cora is the woman who is closest to white in Saint Louis. And she is so white that her difference does not make a difference; indeed, it is more tantalizing. Hence Peyral plunges into this universe of "unknown lust" (42) with this "elegant and perfumed woman" (43). Loti describes the spahi's body as virginal, for until this moment he had never really experienced pleasure. Raised by New Orleans Creoles in an atmosphere of sensual lasciviousness, Cora knows only about vice, pleasure, and wealth. She is older than Peyral and more sexually experienced. It is she who seduces him, who *took* ("avait pris") (45; italics mine) him as her lover, who eventually succeeds in possessing his body and soul. But from time to time, given his inclinations to purity of blood, mind, and soul (to be read: whiteness), Peyral is "revolted" by Cora's "impudeur" (43). He recognizes that Cora and he are fundamentally different, that her love for him has "very little to do with the heart" (44).

A dichotomy is drawn between the heart, mind, and body. While the black is typified by the body and the white by the mind in most literature of the nineteenth century, Loti's well-known sentimentalism necessarily involves the heart. Jean is always thinking (mind), dreaming (mind), reflecting on his feelings (mind), experiencing sexual pleasure (body), and experiencing a profound fondness for his mixed-race mistress (heart), who becomes his "life," his "happiness" (48). Yet Cora is guided by her body's need for satiation. Loti reveals her mindlessness and heartlessness during a climactic scene in which she sexually betrays and dismisses the naive Peyral.

After one exquisite love session, the spahi intuits that his mistress, who rushes him off hurriedly, is seeking gratification in other places. He returns to their love nest to find "someone else had taken his place." Cora has found another lover, a naval officer by the name of Jean. To Jean Peyral Cora does not even look the same; her expression resembles that of a well-known black prostitute he has observed in one of the more unseemly spots in town. At first a *femme élégante*, she has now become a *fille publique*.

Hanging on to the new lovers' every word, Peyral overhears the calculating, sexually voracious Cora declare: "I want you both. I chose you because you are called Jean like him;—without this, I would perhaps have tripped myself up in speaking to him; I am very absent-minded" (54). Deliberately choosing a lover with the same name as Jean, Cora does not want to go through the troubling exercise of remembering, of *thinking*. Easy satisfaction is what she seeks. Her absent-mindedness translates into an absence of mind, which spirals out into an absence of heart:

Cora brusquely advanced toward him—with an expression of a hideous beast that one has bothered during copulation. . . . She closed her door with a gesture of rage, throwing a glass afterward—and all was said. . . . Under the elegant woman with gentle mannerisms, the mulattress, grand-daughter of a slave,[7] reappeared with her atrocious indecency; she had neither remorse, fear, nor pity. (55)

Cora's metamorphosis is complete. Having begun as the *so* white woman with Parisian manners, with a physiognomy hinting at vaguely traceable mixed-race origins, and Creole sensuality, she ends up epitomizing the debased aftereffects of race mixing. She is at once a mindless sexual deviant and an angered copulating beast, atrociously indecent and displaying no pity, sorrow, or fear—in a word, heartless. But all of these dormant characteristics are attributable to her blackness. Loti now scorns Cora by spitting out the racial denomination "femme de couleur" heaped upon her by the *colons* in Saint Louis and by the whites in New Orleans, a description that he felt was unjust to employ initially, given her once "so whiteness."

Underneath the surface of whiteness, one finds abject blackness. Cora, as a mulattress, has taken the best of whiteness in Loti's aesthetics of physical beauty and the worst of the characteristics of blackness: innate vice, dishonesty, mindlessness, and obscene cruelty. She is an ignoble savage. Her duality is further explored when the duped Peyral concludes that she loved both Jeans, since she was "treated as a goddess by the spahi . . . treated by the other as a whore" (86). In effect, the goddess/whore cliché takes on a racial cast. The spahi Jean treated Cora like a goddess, a madonna, like an almost-white woman, while the naval officer Jean treated her as she was — like a *femme de couleur,* a whore like her black compatriots at the unseemly *maisons.* Cora desired both, since both the degradation and veneration seemed to satisfy her bi-racialized psyche. And of course this bizarre satiation can only be carried out by a white male who seems to fulfill his historical patriarchal role of actively exalting the virtues of white femininity and sexually exploiting and denigrating the alleged vices of black femininity.

Peyral's discovery of Cora's treachery brings on a life-threatening fever, exacerbated by the heat of the African sun. He is found in the sand by the "comical negress," Fatou-gaye (49), and is thus saved from being ravaged by vultures. Even after he has spent a lengthy period of recuperation in a hospice, our hero's depression lingers. He receives a timely inspirational letter from his mother, Françoise Peyral. At first he is unable to shake his ennui, for Cora has seemed to place a "heavy veil" over his childhood and family memories (84), but eventually the letter gives him a newfound confidence and allows him to save himself from the precipice of despair. The dark veil slowly recedes; his spirits are eventually buoyed with the coming of spring.

Affected by the heavy air, heat, and the spring mating call of "Anamalis fobil," Peyral comes down with a case of "jungle" fever. Whereas before "he had looked with disgust at this black population: in his eyes they all looked alike . . . the same simian mask, and under that oiled ebony finish, he had not recognized one individual from another" (102), now African women were no longer repugnant to him; he found some ugly, some pretty, some bestial (103). Whereas he had always contrasted black difference with whiteness, he begins to see black differences among black women.

However, this sudden appreciation of black beauty cannot be fully apprehended outside of its narcissistic context. Black difference reverts to a Eurocentered iconography of beauty as Loti asserts that "the negresses had for him a physiognomy in fact like white women" (103). Moreover, the perception of same-difference is not entirely divested of self-serving ends, that is, a libidinal pulsion. All the while dreaming of his fiancée, Jeanne, Peyral needs "someone to help him pass his time of exile" (108). And vowing never again to frequent the houses of pleasure, Peyral's eye-opening realization of black same-difference is brought on by the shortage of white women and a certain dread inspired by the Cora-like mulattresses at the *maisons de jouissance*. The sincerity of Peyral's racial awakening, if you will, is further undercut by Loti's employment of racial and sexual stereotypes over the course of *Le Roman d'un spahi*'s remaining 257 pages.

Given the heat, the air, and the constant beating of the tom-tom for the primitive lovefests, against all of which he is defenseless, the spahi is bound to succumb. This time the spahi *chooses* rather than being *taken*. And since there is always an abundance of readily available, willing, black female sexual partners in Saint Louis for white males, particularly during the mating season, Peyral honors Fatou-gaye. This decision is not taken without inherent feelings of revulsion. Peyral does not want to "rape the little black girls like his comrades" (108); he is also instinctively horrified at the idea of race mixing, knowing that he is "signing a sort of deadly pact with this black race; that the most somber veils were going to descend between him and his mother, fiancée, and memories" (117). He is further terrified by Fatou-gaye's amulets, the sources of some sort of bewitching force. Peyral experiences classic repulsion-attraction symptoms. With each encounter with a black or half-black woman, his memories are partitioned off by a dark veil; he is being further "sullied by contact with black flesh" (263), set apart from who he is: a pure white man. Jean does not have to take Fatou-gaye; she is more than willing. He throws that instinctive white caution to the wind, and the two create a nuptial bed under a baobab tree, to the chanting of Anamalis fobil.

Fatou-gaye is no longer a wild-haired, comical Negress. She has developed into a "gracious" and "charming" young woman. Loti describes her as a "melange of young girl, child, and little black devil, a very bizarre little person" (100). Everything about her is smaller than or less than Peyral: She is a child; he is an adult. She is a young girl of sixteen; he is man of twenty-two. Whereas Peyral's is a godly white existence, she is reduced to a little black devil, "a little monkey girl" (165), "a slave resting at his feet" (124), who reverently addresses him as "mon blanc" (my white man) (130). Fatou-gaye is "indéfinissable" (undefinable) (180), indescribable, bizarre—but not so bizarre as to disturb Peyral's Western sensibilities. Reassuring his French reader, Loti maintains that she has a Grecian face (59):

[She had] a small, narrow, and fine nose with thin nostrils . . . a correct and gracious mouth, with admirable teeth; and then above all large eyes of a bluish finish . . . nothing like the flattened nose and thick-lippedness of certain African people that one usually considers in France as the generic model of the black race. (135)

Fatou-gaye is "very pretty," Loti tells the reader. Her prettiness is derived from her conformity to classical models of beauty, to whiteness, in spite of her blackness.

And although Loti insists upon Fatou-gaye's beauty in the rather backhanded-complimentary way of saying, "She's black, but she's pretty," he cannot resist denigrating and sexualizing the African woman. She may be pretty *like* a white woman, but she is not a white woman. Hence she is inferior, nearly equal to the spahi's yellow "laobé" (179), a dog. Loti invokes the woman as animal motif to characterize the appeal of the Khasson woman to the spahi. She is simultaneously "a monkey, a young virgin, and a tigress" (181). And she demonstrates "absolute devotion to him, the devotion of a dog for its master, the adoration of a nigger for his fetish" (179). His ability to dominate the young African girl, to act out lordship and bondage scenarios, white male master–black female slave dialectics, are at the core of Peyral's affection and disdain for Fatou-gaye. These lordship and bondage scenarios, the taming-of-the-wild-black-woman-as-beast metaphors are viscerally presented when the spahi takes to flogging the young woman with a horsewhip, leaving marks on her nude back (243). To the spahi, these marks begin to form a sort of design, an engraving or writing of his name on the black female's body; they are proprietary marks upon *his* black female slave like the brands used during the era of chattel slavery in the New World.

While Peyral reflects endlessly on his attraction to someone so utterly different from himself, attributing this incomprehensible dilemma to the young woman's amulets, his inertia, and the African air that is so pregnant with sex, in the end Fatou-gaye reassures him of his specialness, his superiority, his maleness, his whiteness. It is these reassurances that allow him to tolerate the *facts* of her existence—that she is "deceitful," a "liar"—"black" (179, 195).

Loti takes great pains to provide the reader with examples of Fatou-gaye's *black* disposition. The spahi begins to tire of the forbidden but delectable sexual trysts, as each encounter begets feelings of disgust with his sensuality and horror at his loss of dignity and the impact on his career mobility because of his taking a Negress as his concubine. His natural, instinctive "great pride" and "white man's dignity" automatically revolt against his weakness for black flesh, against his betrayal of his white "fiancée" for a "little black girl" (180). It is these prideful revolts that precipitate the beatings of Fatou-gaye. The reader is reassured that Fatou-gaye, a masochist of sorts, incites these beatings, for it is the only way, at this juncture in their perverse relationship, that the spahi will touch her.

Fatou-gaye's deceit reveals itself through sexual betrayal. She takes another lover, not a white one, but a "big," "black" Khasson one, one with a "gorilla face" (243). The monkeylike Fatou-gaye appropriately takes a gorilla-faced lover. The assigning of a simian genealogy to the black resonates in *Le Roman d'un spahi*. But also at work is the stereotype, rooted in various natural history tracts such as Buffon's *De l'homme*, Virey's *Histoire naturelle du genre humain*, and Thomas Jefferson's *Notes on the State of Virginia*, surrounding black women's sexual compatibility with apes, monkeys, and gorillas. Pulled into this sexual universe where anything goes, where black gorillas share simianlike women with civilized white men, the spahi cannot but feel disconnected, sullied, exiled. Fatou-gaye acts as a transporter to the primal world. Through his sexual contact with her, Peyral is brought closer to his baser instincts, his less-than-civilized side. He goes through a process of de-evolvement into a world of animality, sexual savagery, and primitivity. This world is no place for a Frenchman.

Peyral finally arrives at this conclusion and terminates his relationship with Fatou-gaye after she sells a watch given to him by his father:

He experienced such despair, the poor Jean, a ripping of his heart. . . . If it had fallen into the sea, or in the river, or into some corner of the desert, but sold, thusly profaned by this Fatou! . . . he had such rage in his heart against this creature. . . . It was this Fatou who for four years took his money, his dignity, his life! . . . In order to keep her, he lost his advancement, all his future as a soldier; for her he remained in Africa, for this little mean and perverse creature with a blackness of soul and face surrounded by amulets and charms. (253)

It is of course the most sentimental of reasons, a father-son affair of the heart, that Loti gives for the ensuing brutal beating Peyral metes out to Fatou-gaye. We, the readers, must comprehend his rage and identify with his hurt, with the ultimate sacrifice of his purity for this thankless, black wretch. Unable to recover the watch from the merchant, Jean Peyral promptly disposes of Fatou-gaye. He throws her belongings into the street; she meekly follows.

Immediately, the hero begins to recover himself; he "finds again

his *white man's* dignity, sullied by the contact with black flesh"
(263). Those past exhilarations, that fever of the senses intensified
by the African climate, now inspire a profound disgust in the spahi
(263). He has re-evolved into *l'homme blanc*. A letter arrives from
his mother, declaring that she has heard news about his dalliances
with a "femme nègre" (267). He receives another letter from Jeanne
Méry that also details his faithlessness. Both letters steel him in his
conviction to never again succumb to the wiles of blackness.

However, Peyral's renewed vows of purity and chastity arrive too
late. Jeanne is married off to a wealthy Frenchman, and his parents are disgraced by his comportment. Heartbroken by the news of
Jeanne's nuptials, the spahi writes to his mother, promising never to
leave his parents again upon his return, and assuring them that they
will find another young woman who wants him. Both mère and père
Peyral and son and future daughter-in-law will live in Jean's idyllic
world, in the village of Cevennes, in the thatched-roof family cottage.

Ordered to ship out for battle, Peyral again encounters Fatou-
gaye. The young woman presents him with his "nearly white" (pres-
que blanc) child (308). His son is tanned ("bronzé") like him and
wears an expression on his small face that seems to beg for an answer
to the perplexing puzzle as to "how his blood of Cevennes found
itself mixed with that of this impure black race" (309). As he easily
falls back into his relationship with Fatou-gaye, the white spahi
forms a family with the black African woman and the *"white"* child
(320). Loti cancels out the child's biological connection to his mother's blackness. It becomes Peyral's son alone. The child has rejected
his mother's blood, the reader is told (308). He questions silently,
that is, via "grave" facial expressions, his father's tragic race-mixing
proclivities (308–9). Although the child is dressed in a boubou and
necklace, the garb of an African child, Loti insists, by italicizing
the word *white*, that he is a *petit blanc*. His hair, unlike that of the
African's, or even that of mulattos, is like his father's. The nameless
white male child is a little Jean Peyral. Thus his mother now has two

white men at whose feet she will sit "like a dog at the feet of its master" (321).

The happiness of Peyral's "little black family" is short-lived (320). The spahi is murdered in the desert by black natives during an ambush; Fatou-gaye, disoriented after discovering the body of her beloved, puts sand in the mouth of the petit blanc and then buries his head in the sand. After killing the child, she places it on its father's chest. The young woman then poisons herself and dutifully awaits her death beside the spahi as birds of prey and native black women who strip corpses of their valuables hover above and on the ground.

Loti concludes his Africanist work with a homage to Peyral's aging parents, who await their son's promised return. As he was dying, the spahi prayed and reminisced about life in Cevennes. Death represents the final dark veil over the spahi's white memories. His earlier hesitations regarding his fate and the signing of a "deadly pact" with blackness have come to fruition. Attempting, through prayer and memory, to will himself into that other world in France in his last living moments, Peyral dies in the burning country of black Africa with his black family, thousands of miles away from France, losing not only his precious white dignity, his white fiancée, his white memories, but eventually (as he lamented in a clever Lotian moment of foreshadowing after Fatou-gaye sold his watch) *his white life.* This is a rather handsome price to pay for race mixing.

The spahi's sexual dalliances with Fatou-gaye did indeed translate into a deadly pact. There is of course no coming back from the physical death that the association with blacks and blackness occasioned. In this Lotian saga, blackness taints, sullies, and eventually murders whiteness. And as if warning his French (male) reader, Loti suggests that in treading upon such dangerous but tempting sexual ground, in crossing that line between purity and impurity, between civilization and the primitive world, between white and black, he risks never returning to his pure state, to whiteness.

Because of the novel's easy affinity for colonialist racial and sexual stereotypes and rather hackneyed analyses of female sexuality, one is apt, without much straining of the imagination, to arrive at the conclusion that the 360 pages of narrative that comprise *Le Roman d'un spahi* yield perhaps the most trite of rules governing white-black sexual relationships, which can be summed up as: once one goes black, one never goes back — to whiteness.

9

Cinematic Venus in the Africanist Orient

Skillfully cultivating her roles as comedian, primitive savage, and black femme fatale through the use of what she called "the intelligence of the body," St. Louis–born Josephine Freda MacDonald, later known as Josephine Baker, took the art of titillating and tantalizing the French imagination to another level. On October 2, 1925, in the first of what would be repeat performances of a wild, two-step dance in the finale of *La Revue nègre*, Baker's "entirely nude" entrance "except for a pink flamingo feather between her limbs" incited, according to one female audience member, Janet Flanner, "an acute response [from] the white masculine public in the capital of hedonism of all Europe — Paris."[1]

Judging from the Africanist influences on Cubism in the 1925 Arts décoratifs exhibition and the African American presence in the 1931 Exposition coloniale, Paris's beau monde, artists, musicians, and general populace had a special affinity for African art and African American jazz and dance. Referred to as the "roaring twenties" in the United States, the 1920s in France were known as *les années folles*. Baker's presence in France could not have been better timed, and the French could not have been better primed. The warm reception that she and other African Americans received in 1920s France was tied both to the heroism of African American GIs in France during World War I and the vivacity of African American cultural expressions such as art, jazz, and dance. Working-class French citizens and café-frequenting intellectuals alike were at one and the same time captivated by American mass culture, namely Hollywood films, and tweaked by their own curiosity regarding the nature of the primitive. The lure of American mass culture further worked to enhance French receptivity to an African American presence in France. Although the French were quite familiar with Africans and Antilleans, because of their slave trading and colonial exploits, African Americans, as descendants of Africans in America, came to signify for them a new sort of black primitivity outside of the *Hexagon* and its colonies. According to Tyler Stovall in *Paris Noir*, "When the French looked at black Americans, they saw a new version of the sensuous, spontaneous African."[2] French exoticism bifurcated to form a specifically African Americanist exoticism that was nonetheless inextricably bound up with Africanism.

Weary of Western scientism and industrialization, which had led, in the minds of many, to various wars, unrest, and social, political, and economic strife, the French stereotypically looked to African Americans as beings who were innocent, sensitive, and primitive, as noble savages persecuted in their own homeland of America, and, finally, as a distraction. France's deteriorating international position and growing national problems made the search for social outlets a priority. Robin Buss writes of the lingering "Mood of the Times" in the aftermath of World War I:

The statistics tell some of the story: 1,400,000 killed, one in 25 of the population, mainly young men; three million wounded; countless numbers bearing the psychological scars of fighting or bereavement. The landscape of northern France was devastated and the economy shattered by war debt and the disruption of industry. . . . Depression followed.[3]

In search of better times, Parisians filled the music halls, nightclubs, cafés, and vaudeville theaters. As a performer in these venues, what Josephine Baker represented in the 1920s and 1930s was not especially different in terms of the ways in which black women had historically been incorporated into the French economy of representation. But unlike Sarah Bartmann, her nineteenth-century in-the-flesh Venus predecessor who also captivated Paris, Baker found personal and economic validation in her constructed primitivity.

Josephine Baker. From Paul Colin's *Le Tumulte noir* Collection. Courtesy of the Smithsonian, Department of Prints and Drawings, Washington, D.C.

Yet she was simultaneously locked into a derogatory and objectified essence of black femaleness. As an entertainer aiming to please her French audiences, Baker realized that her popularity in the 1920s and 1930s undeniably depended on her exploitation of French exoticist impulses, that is, the Black Venus narrative. In her appropriation of the narrative, Baker used her various costumes, ranging from feathers to bananas to a pink muslin *apron,* and her topless and buttock-accentuating dances to toy specifically with feminized, French African–Americanist fantasies. Knowing nothing particularly about Africa, let alone the sexual proclivities of African women, Josephine Baker re-created the Africa, African woman, and African American woman that the French could readily identify as such, along with a "*le jazz hot*" twist. She was a savage sex goddess, a bewitching dark body, a *black*, a *Nègre, Svarta*, Venus, a bundle of raw sensuality, and a happy, innocent child. At one moment, she could, as theater critic André Levinson wrote, perform a "pas de deux sauvage" that "reach[ed] the heights with ferocious and superb bestiality" [4]; at another, she was like "a happy child at play," as Count Harry Kessler from Berlin noted in his journal.[5]

If Josephine Baker's reenactment in the 1920s and 1930s of the essential black female primitive catered to France's need for distraction, so, too, did the rise of colonial cinema in the 1930s. Indeed, after World War I attendance at the French cinema was roughly 250 million and nearly doubled to 402 million by 1945.

French National Cinema and *le cinéma colonial*

The French film industry came into being at the end of the nineteenth century with the production of documentaries and sketches by the likes of Auguste and Louis Lumière, Georges Méliès, and Charles Pathé. Initially heralded as a potential scientific tool because of its ability to capture living subjects, French cinema soon assumed a more prominent role in the popular cultural arena.[6] In Europe and the United States, the film industry experienced rapid growth. From 1895 to World War I France dominated the emerging industry. The war and the following depression took its toll on French film production and the sales of film and film stock, so that shortly after the war only one-third of films shown in France were home-produced and 27.8 percent were imported from the United States.[7] Mourners of the death of the industry found solace in the birth of a national cinema in the 1930s. This period also represented a long-term collaboration with the German film industry. The cinema of the thirties can be characterized as national because it was funded, regulated, and protected by the government and because of its ideological content. (French national cinema continues to be tied to the state; as such, it functions as a state apparatus with all of the ideological baggage that that entails.) On the whole, the national cinema of the thirties served both an ideological and entertainment/escapist role, shoring up the idea of a country united by culture and language as well as allowing a brief getaway—for the duration of a film—from the very real issues of instability, socioeconomic crises, and the rise and spread of fascism in Europe.

In the 1930s, the birth of the national cinema also coincided with the introduction of sound and dubbing. The development of sound made it necessary for the French government to institute protectionist measures so as to regulate the number of imported films screened in France (American films in particular). Since language is critical to the shaping of a national culture, an identity, a sense of nation*ness,* dubbing was crucial, on some level, to preserving specific cultural codes. If one recognizes that cinema generally mirrors the community in which it is produced,[8] it is also evident that the French quota system, through its policing function, was critical to maintaining French cultural hegemony.

Le cinéma colonial of the 1930s seemed to perfectly fulfill the ideological and escapist goals of national cinema. As Pierre Sorlin notes, pinning down the definition of colonial cinema can be a difficult and slippery process.[9] For our purposes, however, colonial films may be described as those feature-length films whose plots revolve around the colonies and have overt or subtle political themes. As with Sorlin, geography and political contexts shape our definitions of colonial cinema. The French were very "fond of 'their' Empire."[10] Hence "Between 1911 and 1962, 210 feature-length films were filmed in the Maghreb."[11] Of the sixty-two feature-length colonial films shot between 1930 and 1939, well over half were filmed partially or totally in North and sub-Saharan Africa.[12]

Colonialist cinematic narratives, like their novelistic and ethnographic counterparts, are never divorced from discourses of power; domination and submission are embedded in empire films' iconographic and narrative features. As a "social lubricant," colonial cinema and the images depicted therein "facilitated new social relationships," that is, France's relationship with itself, "and solidified old ones": France's dominance in relation to its empire.[13] In the Legionnaire genre of colonial films in particular, where the French army, a symbol of patriotism and noble deeds, represents a unified France, one sees this politics at work. The French could cinematographically travel to France *d'outre mer,* flex their colonial muscle — a muscle in the stages of atrophy on European terrain — and simultaneously be reassured of French cultural, racial, moral domination via reinforcement of stereotypes of "their" natives (see the films *Les Hommes nouveaux* [1936] and *La Bandera* [1936]).

As Steven Ungar notes by way of Pierre Leprohon, "The phantasmatic function of an exotic cinema was less one of conveying authentic images of the colonies than of providing the Frenchman with noble actions or satisfying a need for drama and passion that life in France did not provide on an everyday basis."[14] Serving, in most cases, as propaganda for continued colonial expansion, *les missions civilisatrices* (civilizing missions), films like *L'Aventurier* (1934) and *L'Argent* (1936) bolstered the idea of the colonies as promised lands of opportunity (both sexual and economic), adventure, and mystery for the colonialist; this picture was marred only by the presence of shiftless natives, since the "reality" depicted in such films constituted a "confirmation of the most frequent clichés" of the empire and of the *métropole*.[15] The natives represented what the French were not — savage, uncivilized, devoid of culture, highly sexual, closer to nature, irresponsible, and often violent — and what they hoped, during these years of international and national insecurity, they would never become — disempowered, marginal, weak.

A Black Princess in Paris,
A Black Savage in the Africanist Orient

By the time she appeared in *La Folie du jour, La Revue des revues,* and the feature film *La Sirène des tropiques,* Josephine Baker was already a cultural icon. When she returned from her two-year world tour in 1930, the live theater industry was somewhat faltering, as a consequence of the advent of sound, which had revolutionized the film industry. By then, Baker had learned to speak French. Thus her transition from the music hall to the "talking" cinema was an easy one. Because of the rise of colonial cinema, she could easily be read on screen as a black female native from a French colony. The use of stereotypes in empire films all but guaranteed the evocation of the Black Venus narrative. Working hand in glove, the Black Venus narrative and le cinéma colonial landed Baker, or at least the characters that she portrayed, that is, Zou Zou and Aouina, in a series of positions that maintained French metropolitan interests. Baker's renown as a musical comedienne and femme fatale, and the popularity of musical comedies in the 1930s, combined with the colonial film genre to reproduce Baker as a savage, sensual, infantilized cinematic Venus. In dire need of civilizing, the Baker cinematic Venus became a synecdoche for the colonies' savage and sensual state, a Frenchman's paradise ripe for continued conquest. Simply put, Baker/Aouina personifies an unruly Africa.

It is particularly in her second "talking" film, *Princesse Tam Tam* (1935),[16] directed by Edmond Gréville and costarring Albert Préjean as the love interest and Germaine Aussey as the blond female rival, that one clearly sees the Baker-as-sensual-savage-colony motif at work. The film script is very thin on substance and thick on stereotypes. Although the director of the film is Edmond Gréville, Giuseppe "Pepito" Abatino, Josephine Baker's longtime Sicilian lover, manager, and, more important, the creative force behind the international Baker image before World War II, had a significant hand in the production of the film.

Princesse Tam Tam moves between French colonial North Africa (Tunisia) and Paris. In keeping with the North African location, Baker has an Arabic name, Aouina, and is dressed *à l'Orient*. Despite her orientalist name, dress, and the North African location of the film, Baker is racially situated as a black African. At the film's beginning and climax, an Africanist presence is spliced into the sequences immediately preceding or following Baker's appearance. As part of the unruly, sandy landscape, Baker makes her debut by poking her head out of a patch of wild cacti, then running aimlessly along to a pasture where sheep and horses idly graze. She snuggles a sheep and then picks it up, gliding across the white sand with the animal on her back. Thus the spectators' first glimpses of "Africa" consist of miles of sand, dunes, cacti patches, mountainous ranges, beautiful clear skies, and a carefree female savage. Here barefoot native women run with the animals and play "hide-and-seek" in the lush countryside. With no responsibility and no rules to adhere to, native existence, albeit riddled with poverty, as one of the film's actors reports, signifies freedom. French viewers are able to pleasurably contemplate and contrast this uninhibited, disorderly way of life with the order of their world in France.

Aouina ekes out this "carefree" life by begging in the streets and stealing from local café owners. She is discovered by an aristocratic, celebrated Parisian novelist, Max de Mirecourt. Uninspired by his civilized surroundings, bored with his wife's stuffy milieu and haranguing, and suffering from writer's block, de Mirecourt decides to travel to the colonies with his buffoonish sidekick and collaborator, Coton. Coton refers to himself as a "slave" and a "nègre." Although Coton is white, he *slaves* away to help de Mirecourt's like a nègre plowing cotton/*coton* on a Southern plantation for his master. In the colonies, de Mirecourt will certainly find something to stir his "emptied" (vidée) imagination. Upon leaving his wife Lucie and civilized France, Max bellows, "Let's go to the land of the savages, among the real savages. Yes! To Africa! To Africa!" Africa is paradise lost and discovered by the Frenchman, a playground for the imagination, a field of dreams, to which the colonialist will run "for a little while from his ritualized, polite civilization."[17]

The characters do indeed go to Africa, but they go specifically to North Africa. Throughout the film, however, sub-Saharan Africa, North Africa, the Orient, the East, and India are all evoked and conflated into an Africanist Orient. And Aouina/Baker, who will be referred to or cinematographically inscribed varyingly as the Princess of Parador (in allusions to the Orient), a black princess, and Princess Tam Tam (in allusions to sub-Saharan Africa), will represent all those peoples and places that are not civilized or *Civilisation*, as Max's novel is eventually titled, that are imagined as that savage cultural *métissage* that is the Africanist Orient.

In this picturesque "land of savages," where eastern music rings out conspicuously and Arab men or white men in Arab face and native children move about like backdrops in an oriental bazaar, the gaminlike Aouina frolics with children and animals. As a child of nature, she imitates and chases monkeys up trees. A child at heart and in mind, Aouina finds her playmates among the animals and other native children, who, in the service of the film's colonial documentary function, are repeatedly profiled. Moving from one smiling little face to another, the camera allows the French viewer to gaze upon the "real happy savages" of its Empire. Surrounded by native children, the comedienne Baker playfully twists her body and face, to the delight of her audience in the film (the native children) and in the theaters of Paris. At the same time, the attention of the French spectator is drawn to Baker's/Aouina's "exotic" beauty, highlighted by the camera's soft-filtered long takes of a youthful Baker with pencil-thin eyebrows, heavily made-up doe eyes and long, false eyelashes, and a smiling or childishly pouting mouth. The camera expertly captures and disseminates the formula of untouchable "infantilo-innocence that [keeps] the spectator suspended between fantasy and desire."[18] Baker's untouchability is also racialized. On screen, even Josephine Baker could not transcend (much to her well-documented chagrin) cultural taboos relating to white male–black female romantic relations. She could never "win" the affections of the white filmic hero, particularly since her *rivals* were blond French-women. Such a coup would destabilize categories of difference and racially feminized hierarchies that are deeply embedded in — indeed, the bedrock of — the colonialist cinematic narrative.

Aouina's spontaneity, her proximity to "la nature," captivates the writer when he spots her at a café stealing oranges. She tells de Mire-court that her name is Aouina, which means "small source." This is precisely what Aouina will become: a small source of pleasure for the blocked writer, inciting him to uncontrollable laughter, spark-ing his curiosity and imagination so that he will eventually write a best-selling novel, and reconciling him with his bourgeois wife. Using Aouina as his muse, de Mirecourt will write an interracial story ("une histoire de race") in which he says "that he loves her." This story will make a "roman très à la page" (quite a chic novel).

De Mirecourt wants to study Aouina, educate her in the ways of civilization, and then record her "reactions" in order to give the work a degree of authenticity. "This little animal," he states matter-of-factly, "moves me." "She is so naive." Like the nineteenth-century scientific treatises of natural history on the order of Cuvier's study of Sarah Bartmann, this modern novel on the Other will employ the "objective" scientific realism of ethnography. And also like those scientific tracts, the novel will blend a bit of fact with fiction.

As the writer and his white nègre collaborate on the novel and record each of Aouina's reactions, de Mirecourt is receiving a French journal by courier. The scuttlebutt in the society page is that his wife is consorting with the Don Juan–like maharaja from Daetane who collects women like "papillons" (butterflies). Lucie de Mirecourt shrewdly "compromises" herself with the maharaja, a French actor in "Indian face" bedecked in jewels and turban, in order to force her husband to return to civilization and to his senses. In a jealous tan-trum, de Mirecourt vows to finish the novel in one night. The remain-der of *Princesse Tam Tam* is filtered through the writerly imagination, through the novel — *Civilisation* — in which the Other will be pro-

ductively put to use to reinforce continued colonial expansion, race
and class stratifications, and French cultural hegemony and identity.

In the course of the film, Aouina the peasant is transformed into a
princess. She has learned to walk in shoes, play the piano, eat with a
knife and fork, and complete multiplication tables. The filmic novel
then shifts to Paris, where Lucie de Mirecourt has been informed by
Coton that her husband has arrived in the city with a Black Princess ("une princesse noire"), the Princess of Parador, from "a tribe
in Central India," who agreed to come to Paris to allow herself to
be civilized ("se civiliser") for the love of de Mirecourt. Aouina's
blackness sets the Manichaean nature of the filmic novel further on
its course. Baker/Aouina is subjected to racist and sexually racist
invectives throughout the film. Her degraded difference manifests
itself initially on the level of discourse: she deferentially addresses
the French as *vous,* while they, ever cognizant of her racial, cultural,
and class differences, fix her in her subordinate place with *tu.*

Before she is even presented to Parisian high society, the mention
of Aouina's race conjures up images of savagery ("une sauvage")
and cannibalism ("une cannibale"). When a picture of Aouina is featured in the "Who's Who" pages of a paper, disparaging comments
about her nose and that mouth ("Regardez son nez et cette bouche!")
and her "goggled-eyes" are parceled out to console Lucie. "She must
have arrived nude," suggests one of Lucie's female acquaintances,
portrayed by the actress Viviane Romance.

Tired of the polite rituals of civilization, Aouina feigns fatigue
one night so that she can go where the "real" people have "fun,"
where you can "do and say what you want." In civilization, there
are rules and decorum, while in the savage land one runs about
willy-nilly, unconstrained by social mores. The filmic novel blends
the discourses on race, gender, and class. The black female savage
is more at home with the "real" people (read: the working class,
drunks, sailors, and blacks). Drinking rather heavily and cavorting
comfortably with a colorful arrangement of real people at a sailors'
bar (including a white woman in blackface), the princess begins to

sing about the "pleasures" and "desires . . . 'neath the African sky" ("sous le ciel d'Afrique"). Aouina/Baker then dances her trademark Charleston, smiling and playfully kicking her legs in the air. This is the first time in the film that Aouina/Baker is explicitly sexualized and sexual. Africa is a continent where love, sexual desire, and endless pleasure are allowed to flourish underneath its skies. As if it were a modernist Club Med, Africa is imagined as having *bouffer,* *baiser,* and *bronzer* as its reasons for being; these are its gifts to Western man. With such salacious advertisements, it is no wonder that the "French were so fond of 'their' empire." Moreover, it is from the mouth of a savage that Africa's raisons d'être, already entertained in the French imagination, are made known.

Spied by Viviane Romance, who we should obviously conclude was slumming at the sailors' bar, Aouina is described as behaving in a manner unbecoming a princess in a report to Lucie: "She was doing a savage dance" ("Elle faisait . . . une danse de sauvage"). Lucie, in relating the details of Aouina's danse de sauvage to the maharaja, suggests that she behaved like a prostitute ("une fille"). Here again the savage is sexualized in the most degraded terms. In a throwback to the nineteenth century, the relationship between black female sexuality and prostitute sexuality is revisited. Aouina is further rebuked for leading a double life ("une double vie"): noble savage by day, *ig*noble savage by night.

Aouina's danse de sauvage at a black-tie affair represents the filmic novel's climax. Coton, Aouina, and de Mirecourt are invited to a party hosted by the maharaja. As part of a scheme to embarrass Max and reveal Aouina for what she really is — "a savage," "a cannibal," and "a prostitute" — Lucie wants to entice the princess into performing another round of this savage dance. De Mirecourt, in the following scene, warns Coton to make sure Aouina does not slip up (read: fall back into savagery) at this very important event. After all, she has been caught eating with her hands and demonstrating a bit too much excitement at social events such as the horse races.

Aouina is nonetheless left to her own vices: drink and dance. At the social she is approached by Lucie's confidante. Plying her with drink, she notices that Aouina is particularly enthralled by the beating of tom-toms by an African drummer. It is the call of the wild to the wild, a savage code that only another savage can decipher. "How can you resist?" she asks provocatively. Aouina/Baker cannot. She leaps onto the stage and strips and dances about wildly, to the socialite guests' delight. The camera moves between Baker and the African drummer. The African who was flashed at the opening of the film is not really in the film or among the film's actors. He has been intercut in these sequences for racial affect. As she is contrasted with the shirtless, chanting African drummer, the French spectator sees the real Aouina. She is not the Princesse de Parador, which they already knew, but rather Princesse Tam Tam.

In the end Aouina, who has never really left the savage land or fallen in love with the writer, is shown with Tahar, a white actor in shadowy and menacing Arab face, and their Africanist oriental child in the villa left by de Mirecourt. What was once an impeccably decorated villa is now overrun with chickens, goats, and cows. Books are carelessly tossed about. One of the books on the floor is a personally autographed copy of de Mirecourt's *Civilisation*. A smiling Aouina looks on as a cow chews the book's title page.

A semblance of order is restored at the film's end. When Coton wishes Aouina were in France to celebrate the novel's success, de Mirecourt remarks: "Aouina est bien où elle est" (Aouina is fine where she is). Civilization emerges intact, as do the sensual savage colonies. Chaos cannot be introduced into the order of civilization, just as order has not fully subdued chaos, thus necessitating continued civilizing missions. According to Freud on the matter of jokes, one has to peer behind jokes/comedies for their real meanings. What they say is not often what they mean; indeed, they mask something else. Likewise, *Princesse Tam Tam*, though a colonial musical comedy, tells us more concerning the French's attitudes about themselves, their desires, and their fears. The colonies are reassuringly primitive, despite French civilizing missions; they will always be savage, sensual, childlike. French assimilationist concepts, such as *evolué* and the *devenir français* process, prove at best bankrupt and specious. For if they were not, where would civilized men turn for reassurances of their superiority, for reinforcements of their identity, for creative stimuli, to bouffer, bronzer, and baiser? The colonies are there to "provide a little human sustenance" so as to allow a reconnection with the self when the French become "too mechanized."[19] And as Aouina, the quintessential female savage, as Black Venus, Josephine Baker used her "intelligence of the body," her exoticist acumen, to create a vehicle through which that human sustenance could be tapped.

EPILOGUE

Because each had discovered years before that they were neither white nor male, and that all freedom and triumph was forbidden to them, they had set about creating something else to be. — Toni Morrison, *Sula*

For ourselves, and for humanity . . . we must turn over a new leaf, we must work out new concepts, and try to set afoot a new [wo]man. — Frantz Fanon, *The Wretched of the Earth*

In this work I have attempted to situate black female personae in the thick of the nineteenth- and twentieth-century literary, scientific, and cultural imagination. In conclusion I would like to shift the focus to black women's efforts, particularly those by Francophone Caribbean women, in the words of bell hooks, "to make the oppositional space where [their] sexuality can be named and represented, where [they] are sexual subjects — no longer bound and trapped."[1] While hooks's discussion refers specifically to Anglophone black feminist cinematic productions of the twentieth century, this primarily literary study will take black women's writerly endeavors, particularly the writings of Haitian Marie Chauvet and Guadeloupean/Senegalese Myriam Warner-Vieyra as its points of departure. In effect, writing represents a critical oppositional space where black women have been able to redefine, indeed reinvent, themselves. The act of writing allows for a return to the self, an exploration of the self. Through "writing," according to French feminist antitheory theorist Hélène Cixous, "women will return to the bodies which have been more than confiscated from [them]."[2]

The unearthing of writings by nineteenth-century Francophone

Antillean women is still a developing area of research for archivists and scholars. As Pamela Mordecai and Betty Wilson observe in their coedited anthology of Caribbean women's writings, *Her True True Name:*

Prose works by women in the Caribbean date from the mid–nineteenth century—some may be even earlier—but in the face of poor documentation and archival work that seems at best biased, it would be unwise to make more than general comments on the historical/developmental aspects of the contribution of women prose writers. . . . Jack Corzani in his comprehensive work *La littérature des Antilles-Guyane Françaises* (1978) lists several early French Caribbean women writers who were white.[3]

And Mordecai and Wilson list only one nineteenth-century prose writer of color—an Anglophone writer, Mary Seacole, from Jamaica. The bibliography compiled by Guadeloupean woman writer Maryse Condé in *La Parole des femmes: Essai sur romancières des Antilles de langue française,* a history of writing by Francophone Antillean women, begins in the early twentieth century with Martinican writer Suzanne Lacascade's feminist articulation of negritude in *Claire-Solange* (1924). And the history of French Antillean and Creole writings by Martinican literary theorists Patrick Chamoiseau and Raphael Confiant, *Lettres créoles: Tracées antillaises et continentales de la littérature, 1635–1975,* also situates its first Francophone black woman writer in the twentieth century.

Stories of mythical proportions describing Antillean women's activism nonetheless pervaded the oral histories of the nineteenth century, an era of slavery during which the fine-tuning of the French colonial system was taking place. Tales of resisting women marooned in the mountains of Guadeloupe and Martinique, such as those comprising the saga of Solitude, are legendary in the former colonies.

Born a slave in or around 1772 on the island of Guadeloupe, Solitude was conceived violently during the Middle Passage from Africa to the New World. Her mother was an African and her father a nameless *négrier.* As a young woman, she was sold from plantation to plantation until she fled to the mountains during the brief abolition of slavery in Guadeloupe in 1791. She fought against the French colonial military and the slave-holding and trading classes who attempted to maintain their stronghold on the island and led charges against the army when slavery was reestablished in the colonies by Napoleon. Solitude was executed in November 1802, immediately after giving birth to her daughter.[4]

Solitude's struggle for freedom, her identity as a black woman, and her sexual abuse and sexual subjectivity are the stuff of many contemporary Guadeloupean writers' novellas, notably Simone Schwarz-Bart's *Pluie et vent sur Telumée Miracle* and Maryse Condé's *Moi, Tituba, Socière de Salem.*

It is the continuing, arduous process of recovering nineteenth-century Antillean women's writing that compels us to look toward the twentieth century, a century with a cartographically richer body of writings by Francophone Caribbean women of color.

Because of this diversity among the writers, tied as much to the historical processes of their specific countries as to the complexities and range of experiences articulated within the writings themselves, it is impossible to situate this or that novel as *the* oppositional text of black female representation. This circumstance is of course at the very root of their oppositionality,[5] in that the representations reflect the range and diversity of black female subjectivities rather than monolithic, homogenizing constructions of black femaleness. To be sure, there are thematic and experiential similarities involving such areas as sexual oppression, inter/intraracial conflicts, sexual discovery, male-female relationships, exile, alienation, identity, childhood, and adolescence. But there are differences as well, rooted in individual experiences of the conflicts investigated by the novelist and articulated through the female protagonist.

Candidly revealing the strictures of Haitian society around issues of color, class, gender, race, and sexuality, exiled writer Marie Chauvet helped establish a new literary ground and simultaneously scandalized her family with the 1968 publication by Gallimard of her provocative trilogy *Amour, colère, folie.*[6] Marginalized as a "minor" writer in Haitian letters, Chauvet, according to Haitian critic Yanick Lahens, "because of the sheer power of her themes and the intensity of her style paved the way for the modern novel in Haiti."[7] Chauvet's frank presentation of the repressive sexual, political, and anti-intellectual climate as well as her critique of a colluding Haitian aristocratic class, to which she belonged, led her family to suppress further distribution, translation, and publication of the novel after her death, and to go so far as to purchase all the unsold copies in Gallimard's warehouse.[8]

In the first part of Chauvet's trilogy, *Amour*, the reader is introduced to the female narrator, Claire. Claire suffers in her body; she is the eldest and darkest daughter of three in a privileged social and familial milieu of "blancs et mulatres-blancs" (12). Her name itself contains within it her corporeal conflicts; it is cruelly ironic. She is Claire with "la couleur foncée de peau" (dark skin) (10). As a legacy from her paternal great-grandmother, Claire's blackness sticks out sorely. Even though she questioned whether "she was really their daughter" after looking upon her mother's "milky whiteness" (blancheur laiteuse) (111), she is not particularly conscious of the social weight her difference makes until the subject of marriage is broached. Her father intends to persuade, monetarily, the family of a "white mulatto" to take her hand in marriage. It is then that her younger sister asks: "Mother, why is Claire black?" (119). Refusing to compromise her idea of love, to "buy" a husband in spite of her blackness, Claire undergoes, in Fanonian terms, a sort of "epidermalization of inferiority," without the dimensions of racial self-hatred. Her inferiority complex is a subjective one, consisting of hypersensitivity to allusions to her color. She does not cultivate a distaste for all things black, nor is there a desire for a whitewashing of her body. She merely accepts bitterly the color constraints of society — the devaluation of her person from without because of her color.

Claire, in her turn, vows never to marry. Her precarious condition is further exacerbated by her sexually repressive family, who are guided by the teachings of the Catholic Church. When we meet the narrator, she is thirty-nine and refers to herself as "une veille fille" (an old maid) (9): unmarried, unmarriageable, and a virgin, all owing to the color complexes of Haitian society, which are linked to French colonialism and American imperialism.

While her lack of *claire*ness leads to personal experiences of sexual frustration, unrealizable love, and social marginalization, Claire is the most *clear*-sighted of all the novel's characters. It is through her eyes (when she assumes the role of spy, which she frequently does) that the reader witnesses color and class contradictions, the economic exploitation and marginalization of Haitians from the "morne de lion" (hills), the brutal repression of a dissenting Haitian intelligentsia, the internalization of inferiority and pretentious airs exhibited by a complacent and cowardly aristocratic class of Haitians, and the rise of a terrorizing military class comprised of the darkest blacks.

But particularly fascinating are the passages of *Amour* where Chauvet describes Claire's sexual awakening and desire, which are inspired by the nuptials to a white Frenchman of Félicia, her politically simpleminded "mulâtresse-blanche" sister. Exhibiting daring that has been seen recently in Maryse Condé's *Hérémakhonon* and Antiguan Anglophone writer Jamaica Kincaid's *Lucy* and *Autobiography of My Mother,* Chauvet was way ahead of her time in graphically presenting black female desire. Unlike de Pons's Ourika, who lusts after the Frenchman Charles, Claire does not desire interracial sex as such but only fulfillment. She does not want to take her sister's place as wife to a Frenchman and mother to a mixed-race child, to be a mulâtresse-blanche; rather she wants what she was unfairly denied: *amour.* She is, in every sense of the word, the embodiment of Fanon's colonized [wo]man in *The Wretched of the Earth,* who envies the colonizer, in this case her sister who treats her like a domestic, who wants to eat at the colonizer's table, and sleep with the colonizer's husband.

Hiding pornographic pictures of couples under her bed, masturbating while imagining her younger sister, Annette, frolicking with her brother-in-law, Jean Luze, and dalliances of her own with Jean Luze and the misogynist, sexually impotent dark body of the Ton Ton Macoute Calédu—all these various scenes of seduction titillate

Claire's imagination and allow Chauvet to carefully paint a tableau not of someone who is a sexually depraved hysteric, but rather of a desiring woman forced into repression, forced into hypocrisy because of the racial and sexual strictures of her social class.

Claire reveals the facts of Haitian existence not merely through her eyes, but through her writing, her journal. Writing is Claire's therapy; writing allows her to explore her world and her feelings: "I believe I can write; I believe I can think; I have become arrogant; I have taken consciousness of myself" (10). Through writing, she externalizes the repressiveness of this social world, she takes her "revanche" (revenge) on that world (1).

As a tale of alienation, identity, and madness, Myriam Warner-Vieyra's novel *Juletane* opens with the reading of a now dead Guadeloupean woman's journal by a West Indian nurse who is contemplating marriage to an African. The journal recounts the trials of Juletane, a young college-educated Antillean woman without family who travels with her husband, Mamadou, to his homeland in Africa, only to find that he is a practicing Muslim who follows the polygamous traditions of Islam. Juletane is further marginalized because she is not African; she is referred to by her co-wife, Ndèye, Mamadou's third wife, as a *toubabesse* (a white woman). Unable to assimilate in the patriarchal, polygamous culture, Juletane succumbs to *la folie:* she kills the children of the first co-wife and disfigures the malicious third co-wife, who calls her *la folle.* In the end, Mamadou dies in a car crash, while Juletane dies in a quasi-state of delirium alone in a psychiatric hospital.

Like Claire, Juletane keeps a journal as a form of therapy, to retell her story in her own words. She recognizes the transformative, subjectivizing nature of writing, the power of words: "I allow myself to be taken in by the magic of words . . . to write a journal of my life. . . . I have remained silent for such a long time, living in indifference to things and beings. Today, my only assurance is re-birthing myself to life" (93–94).[9] Like so many other Francophone Caribbean women writers, Warner-Vieyra and Chauvet are attempting to name more than their sexuality by incorporating sexual subjectivity into the interlocking nexus of race, gender, class, color, and their knowledge of colonialism, imperialism, neocolonialism, alienation, and a myriad of other of life's day-to-day public and private experiences. In doing so, they present fuller portraitures than ever before of black women's experiences. They are, in effect, working out new concepts, trying to set afoot new women.

From Solitude's guerrilla activism to Chauvet's tableau of repressed female subjectivity to Warner-Vieyra's tale of madness and therapeutic writing, these subversive revisionings of black women through writing challenge hegemonic inscriptions of black female bodies into reductive, sexualized, and abject narratives, into the cloistering, voyeuristically pleasurable, cramped and, more important, safe space (for the French male writer/director/spectator/reader) of Black Venus.

APPENDIX

The Hottentot Venus, or Hatred of Frenchwomen

Vaudeville in One Act by Théaulon, Dartois, and Brasier

Presented for the first time at the Theater of Vaudeville,

*November 19, 1814**

> *"I would have believed, such is your beauty,*
> *That your fatherland was France"*

CHARACTERS	ACTORS
The Baron	Mr. Hipolite
The Baroness	Ms. Bodin
Adolph, their nephew	Mr. Isambert
Amelia, their niece	Ms. Rivière
The Chevalier d'Ericourt	
Amelia's Parisian suitor	Mr. Séveste
Fanchette, the Baroness's attachée	Ms. Betzi
The Governess	Mrs. Lenoble
Villagers	

The theatrical setting consists of a park entrance at the side of the château and a small pavilion to the right where the actors enter by going up a few steps. The scene is set three leagues from Paris.

*Publisher Chez Martinet, rue du Coq St. Honoré, Paris, 1814. In Bibliothèque Nationale de France, Department of Printed Matter/Microfilm, call number: 8 Yth 18862. The idea for this play was taken from Vade's *La Canadienne*. All translations are mine.

SCENE I

The BARONESS, AMELIA, *and the* GOVERNESS

At the curtain's raising, the Baroness can be seen leaving the pavilion; at the door to the left, one hears three small taps. The Baroness opens the door and Amelia enters and embraces her aunt.

AMELIA You are going to inform me, my dear aunt, why I have had to enter your château so mysteriously; a messenger, a guide at the entrance of the forest, the secret door to the park, the three light taps as signal. . . . In truth, this all resembles a chapter from a novel.

BARONESS You will know the reasons for this mystery soon enough. But first, let us go into this pavilion for which I alone have the key, and where we will not risk any surprises.

(*She opens the pavilion.*)

AMELIA (*removing her veil*) Ah! My dear aunt, allow me to catch my breath a moment. I very much want to be a heroine of a novel, but I must fore-warn you that I love freedom; hence I don't go in for old dungeons or isolated pavilions. Besides, why should I hide myself here? I am a widow, my cousin is unattached; it is, as one says, highly proper. I am beautiful; this marriage is progressing all by itself.

BARONESS It is that which deceives you, my dear Amelia! You should know that Adolph does not even want to see you and that if he learned that you were at the château, he would leave immediately.

AMELIA Ah, well! What a charming cousin I have here. Why did you seem to desire that I cast my lot with his? You described him as a very amiable young man. I took you at your word. I consented to all, and then I arrive to receive the most cruel insult that one could pay to a lovely woman. It is to hear someone say: "He does not want to see you."

BARONESS When I had my nephew come from the depths of Languedoc, and I had planned this nuptial bond, I overlooked the fact that Adolph was touched by madness.

AMELIA How, my aunt? My cousin has lost his reason! I am surely not the one who will be able to render him reasonable — let me inform you of this.

BARONESS I have however counted upon you, Amelia.

AMELIA I thank you, my aunt.

To the tune of *Vaudeville de la belle fermière*[†]

I love novels of intrigue,

And already all of this mystery

Promises me one of the happiest,

Where I will appear I hope.

Should it become necessary to languish,

Whimper

Pity someone

Repent

Hate

Run

Suffer

Die,

My aunt, I imagine,

Would have chosen another heroine.

I see that we have to fool my cousin; tell me of this.

BARONESS Yes, we must deceive him in order to make him happy; Adolph was born with an ardent imagination and experienced love before acquiring that judgment which should have guided his choice. He was pitilessly betrayed.

AMELIA In all truth, my aunt, there are some women who are simply treacherous.

BARONESS Adolph loved madly . . . as one loves at his age! Imagine his sadness! . . . Finally, the time came to ease his pains; he made another choice.

AMELIA Was he betrayed this time?

BARONESS Like the first time.

[†] All song titles are given in the original French.

AMELIA I would have wagered so! This poor cousin! And since that time he has sworn an eternal hatred for all women?

BARONESS No; for all Frenchwomen.

AMELIA He doesn't have any nationalist spirit!

BARONESS And without having renounced marriage altogether, he has made a vow to only marry a woman absolutely foreign to our customs and morals.

AMELIA You mean, a savage?

BARONESS Precisely. It is my dear husband who, since his return from America, rouses his imagination by vaunting of morals that he does not know and of women he has never seen.

AMELIA How I am longing to embrace this dear uncle! I was very young when he left France! He has made, one says, a tour of the world?

BARONESS Him! He has only made the crossing from the Orient to Guadeloupe. But his imagination has traveled for him, and if it were not a bit of stupidity that convinced him of his sighting of some savages in the Adriatic sea, he should be able to pass for a great traveler; he lies with inconceivable boldness! Listening to him, one would think he knows all the languages, every country.

AMELIA But he is the most formidable of opponents that I will have had to combat!

BARONESS Does this already frighten you?

AMELIA

To the tune of *Vaudeville de jadis et aujourd'hui*
Under such circumstances
One can always count on me.
I see that it is necessary to exercise prudence
But my heart feels no terror.
A woman of our era
Knows of her triumphant power.

I may be wary of men
But they have never scared me.

BARONESS
I love this noble daring;
Soon we will have need of it.
However, take guard, my niece,
That it does not carry you too far.
The prudent rarely fall
Within the traps of a seducer.
All the women who succumb
Are those who have never feared.

AMELIA Rest at ease, my aunt, I shall not succumb.

BARONESS God willing!

BARON (*backstage*) Hey! Tallyho! . . . .

BARONESS I hear my husband. Good! He is with Adolph; they are going hunting; Let's go into that pavilion to decide on our plan.

To the tune of *Je regardais Madelinette*
Friendship alone fuels us,
No one will blame us;
And when you will be his wife,
Adolph will thank us.

AMELIA
As for deceiving him, I hope
To show here all my talents;
It is my cousin! One has surely to do
Something for his parents.

AMELIA *and* BARONESS
Friendship alone fuels us.

(*They enter the pavilion.*)

SCENE II

The BARON, ADOLPH, *in hunting attire*

ADOLPH What, my dear uncle, having no sooner arrived, you are already dreaming of again leaving?

BARON Yes, my friend, since peace is about to reopen the seas, I want to go visit all my American possessions.

ADOLPH You are my only defender here. If you leave, my aunt is going to torment me again on the subject of my marriage, and you know, above all, my feelings.

BARON Yes, I know that you do not want a Frenchwoman; you must have an exotic one, and I applaud your resolve.

ADOLPH I was so disgracefully deceived!

> To the tune of *Signale d'un galant négligé*
> Yes, from Frenchwomen henceforth
> I want to flee the cruel empire.
> Alas! They have never known
> But to destroy the heart that allows itself seduced.
> To hate them is where my hope lies;
> I hate them, but such are their charms,
> That in order not to give them arms,
> I shall not see them.

BARON It is true that except for Native American women and Hottentots, I have not seen any who are prettier. Avoid them with care until my return. I promise to search for the woman you want, if I have to scour the four corners of the globe.

> To the tune of *Je suis colère et boudeuse*
> In order to give you a wife
> In keeping with your fancies
> I want to
> Visit thousands of countries like young Peyrouse.

From the coasts of Barbary
I will go to Greenland,
To Mesopotamia
And to the Island of Ceylon.
I will see the Iroquois,
The young girls of Goa,
All the Chinese beauties,
Those of Anaamoka;
I will study Indian women
All the diverse caprices,
I will see Canadian women;
I will observe their foibles;
I will learn from the Visigoths
Qualities, Faults.
If I see the Hottentots,
I will write you two words of them.
And if the object of your passion
Was not in Persia,
I will search for your wife
In the empire of the crescent.

ADOLPH (*laughing*) Much obliged, my uncle, but if you would just find her somewhere.

BARON Here or elsewhere, it is always the same thing.

ADOLPH

To the tune of *Honneur, vaines grandeurs!*
Let's go, Let's go hunting
It was always the true pleasure of the wise.

BARON

It is a pleasure that does not tire me.

ADOLPH

For me, I take pleasure
In the depths of the forest:

Here, quite far from beautiful women
And from faithless women,
I know, with sadness,
How to brave their contempt.

BARON

Come take your revenge on them
Upon the rabbits.

CHORUS

Let's go, let's go hunting. . . .

SCENE III

AMELIA *alone*

She leaves the pavilion. During the preceding scene she has observed and overheard Adolph by the window.

AMELIA Ah! My little cousin, you have very extravagant ideas! You must have a woman who comes from faraway climates! A savage! We will see, we will see.

To the tune of *Vers le temple de l'hymen*
From today on, I aim
To convert you through my finesse;
I hope by my address
To subdue you in little time.
This venture is brilliant!
For a young innocent woman
Still well naive
It will be embarrassing
To undertake such a task;
But once one is a widow
One knows how to go about it.

The CHEVALIER (*in the wings or backstage*) Everyone is in the garden, and I have come across no one. This is charming! This is delicious!

AMELIA Who is it I hear? It is the Chevalier d'Ericourt, the most persistent of my admirers from Paris.

SCENE IV

AMELIA *and the* CHEVALIER

CHEVALIER At last, I meet you, my beautiful one! I want to die! I did three-quarters of a league in this park to find you! If I had known this, I would have come here with my buggy.

AMELIA You here, Chevalier, in the countryside, far from Paris!

CHEVALIER It is extraordinary, it is true; but I cannot be where you are not.

AMELIA You have certainly chosen badly the moment to show fidelity.

CHEVALIER How? That which has been related is thus true? What a disaster!

> To the tune of *On dit que je suis sans malice*
> When I saw melancholy
> In your face replacing passion,
> When your amiable gaiety
> gave way to gravity;
> When I saw you, Amelia,
> Fleeing all the pleasures of life,
> From that time on, I would have bet
> That you were going to marry.

AMELIA You would have certainly lost your bet.

CHEVALIER No, no, I would have won, I am sure of it. But, charming Amelia, Adolph is not suitable for you. He will bury you with his love in the middle of some desert in some gothic château. As a husband you need an amiable man who knows how to appreciate all your beautiful qualities, which make you shine in Paris, and that man, he is me!

AMELIA You?

CHEVALIER Me! I do not know if it is mere sympathy, but for some days a giddiness about marriage has taken hold of me! I must marry, and if you do not marry me, you will be the reason that I will undertake some folly.

AMELIA I prefer that you, rather than me, were responsible for it.

CHEVALIER You are thus abandoning Paris?

AMELIA I am not saying that.

CHEVALIER Never was it more agreeable.

> To the tune of *de la Trenitz*
> At this moment Paris
> Is a charming sojourn:
> The traces of misfortune
> Are covered by flowers.
> The past is forgotten,
> One enjoys the present,
> And one sees in the future
> only pleasure.
>
> At last, full of assurance,
> The shopkeeper moves forward,
> Guided by the hope
> Of enriching his children.
> The painter readies himself,
> The poet composes,
> The warrior reposes,
> The arts are triumphant.
> From abroad especially
> One sees everywhere
> The immense crowd;
> Because all the countries
> Find themselves, I think,
> In Paris.
> Each one follows happily
> His custom

And his dress,
That which often makes
The most striking contrast.

Our more energetic theaters
Are already very clever;
All our famous actors
Loaded with money, honors
Crowned with laurels
Go to their homes
Where repose
Relieves them from their work.

To the French it is revealed
That being prepared is new play with zeal,
For more than six months,
Society's crème de la crème
To the Mona Lisa
From all parts abound,
And no one protest
Its saucy tone.

A Dog
Much
Praised
At the Gaîté
Makes one sob:
Depending on their desires
There is something for everyone;

the most
Popular,
The Hottentot Venus,
Among the theatergoers
Competes only with the Boxers.

To the voice of pleasure

> You must obey;
> Return to Paris
> In the bosom of games, of laughter:
> It is here that beauty
> Commands in freedom;
> It is there, I believe,
> That you should hand down laws.

AMELIA This is a striking tableau; it must be especially interesting to see a Hottentot woman.

CHEVALIER A woman! She is a Venus, madam! A Venus who has arrived here in France from England, and who, at this moment, incites the admiration of all connoisseurs.

AMELIA So she is beautiful?

CHEVALIER Oh! Of a frightening beauty.

> To the tune of *Une fille est un oiseau*
> Really, this is no game!
> Already all Paris praises her.
> This woman is amazing:
> First she speaks very little.
> Her song seems barbarous,
> Her dance is lively and burlesque,
> Her face a little grotesque,
> Her waist of a becoming contour.
> They say that marriage binds her;
> But this Venus, I wager,
> Will never inspire love.

AMELIA Chevalier, no doubt they speak of her a great deal?

CHEVALIER It is a question only of her. . . . She has some little Hottentot songs that are so gay! She takes little Hottentot steps that are so light, and in Paris they so cherish all that which is exquisite. All our ladies have already ordered for this winter dresses and overcoats in Hottentot styles.

AMELIA (*aside*) This idea is bizarre. We will perform a comedy at my aunt's home.

To the tune of *Nous accourons*
My project
Is
Perfect;
Of its effect
I am laughing beforehand;
I have already the assurance
Of a success
The most complete.

CHEVALIER
Please explain? . . .

AMELIA
During this stay,
I find you most agreeable;
But, forever,
Forget your love.
I hope one day
To render you reasonable . . .

CHEVALIER
I sensed that.
Don't count on it.

TOGETHER

AMELIA	CHEVALIER
My project, etc.	So what
	Is this project
	Which gives her so much assur-ance
	And promises her beforehand
	A success
	The most complete?

CHEVALIER
I will change
Your rebellious soul,
Whether you like it or not.
I will make you feel compassion,
I will succeed
In making you loyal.

AMELIA
I sensed that.
Don't count on it.

TOGETHER

AMELIA	CHEVALIER
My project, etc.	What is, etc.

AMELIA *exits*

SCENE V

CHEVALIER (*alone*) This woman does not love me. What a shame! She is pretty, rich. Me, I have nothing. We were perfectly suitable for one another. But it doesn't matter. I have made up my mind to get married; it is important that I realize this little fantasy.

To the tune of *En amour comme en amitié*
Mohammed, your charming precepts
Must not encounter rebels;
When you allow your happy children
To tie the knot with all the beautiful girls.
In France, where one sees so many charms
Shared among the damsels,
If one were able to have many wives,
Ah! How I would marry many!

SCENE VI
CHEVALIER *and* FANCHETTE

FANCHETTE (*enters in tears*)

To the tune of *La danse n'est pas que j'aime*
Alas! The dance is all that I love,
And more marriages in the château!
Dancing is such a wonderful pleasure!
With extreme politeness
A young man invites me to dance;
He takes me by the hand, leading me, ...
Ah! how I pity
Those women who do not dance.

CHEVALIER (*approaches Fanchette*) The little natural. But she is jewel, this child here. Oh goodness, pardon me! I believe that she is crying. What is wrong, beautiful child?

FANCHETTE Oh! Nothing, sir!

CHEVALIER Come on, nothing? And you are crying!

FANCHETTE These tears are not for me.

CHEVALIER Oh! For whom then?

FANCHETTE It is for a young woman to whom has been delivered the greatest affront. Her aunt has brought her here to marry her cousin.

CHEVALIER Adolph!

FANCHETTE As it happens, all was being readied for the wedding, and then the cousin refused to marry her; he does not even want to see her.

CHEVALIER In truth! Ah, ah, ah! This is delicious.

FANCHETTE The woman will not have a husband and we will not have a dance. This is why I am crying, in pity for her and sadness for me.

CHEVALIER You are compassionate.

FANCHETTE

To the tune of *Vaudeville de Partie carrée*
Yes, I really sympathize with her disgrace,
And I am not afraid to show my sorrow:
It is that which you are seeing; if I were in her
place,
I don't know what I would do.
She so believed, me I supposed thus,
That she was taking a husband of her taste!
It is cruel, when one counts on something
To not have anything at all.

CHEVALIER Ah, ah! He has thus flatly refused.

FANCHETTE Flatly! The Baron, his uncle, has promised to marry him to a woman. How could he do this? A savage woman! A savage woman! It must be a joke. Where does one find one?

CHEVALIER (*aside*) She is very pleasing. (*Aloud*) Savage women?

To the tune of *Le Briquet*
Their country, I swear to you,
Is not very well known to me,
because I have never seen it.
I do know that nature
Has given them health,
Force and agility,
Sometimes pride.
Some claim that they are beautiful,
But according
To scientists,
Savage women are very often
Wild and cruel.

FANCHETTE Ah! My god, this country must be far from Paris.

CHEVALIER (*aside*) Adolph wants to marry a savage! He certainly has some taste; this is the gift to present him. (*Aloud*) My dear, run after your master. Tell him that I am leaving, but that he will see me today, that he should not finish anything without me. I assure you that if he does not have himself a marriage here, this evening, it will not be my fault. (*Aside*) If through such means the young widow is going to stay with me!

FANCHETTE Really, Mr. Adolph is going to be married?

CHEVALIER Yes, my pretty, and while waiting, take this kiss. (*He tries to kiss her.*)

FANCHETTE (*pinches him*) Oh! Stop it!

CHEVALIER But I believe you have pinched me, little savage.

FANCHETTE What did you call me, savage? Understand this, mister, I am no more savage than another.

CHEVALIER Ah, ah, ah! Calm down, my dear child! You are too pretty to be a savage. Word of honor, it would be a shame for us!

FANCHETTE And for me as well?

CHEVALIER

To the tune of *Comme ça vient, comme ça passe*
Oh Good folly!
Without me, without my cunning,
Your master, I bet,
Might have remained a bachelor.

FANCHETTE

All the girls are going to be happy!

CHEVALIER

I love to make men happy,
And even more so women!

FANCHETTE

You are a special man.

CHEVALIER   FANCHETTE

Oh good folly! etc. . . . Etc. . . .

CHEVALIER

For the upcoming wedding
Get all the girls ready!

FANCHETTE

They will not be late!
They will arrive rather too early.

CHEVALIER

Such a joke gives me promise.

FANCHETTE

What fun I shall have!

CHEVALIER

Ah! You are going, this evening,
To dance!

FANCHETTE

To waltz!
If I was getting married,
Me, I would never stop,
Ever.

TOGETHER

O good folly, etc.

(*The Chevalier leaves.*)

SCENE VII

The BARONESS *in the pavilion;* ADOLPH *arrives while reading.*

ADOLPH

To the tune of *De Doche*
At the mercy of my whims,
Oh how much I want

To spend my life
In the bosom of your forests,
On faraway and wild banks
That have not yet
For our magnificent customs
Changed your golden age.

BARONESS There he goes into one of his obsessions.

ADOLPH Heroic Atala, every time that I reread the touching tales of your loves, I regret not having been born on the banks of the Orinoco or in the savannas of Florida.

BARONESS Poor young man. It is high time to come to your aid.

SCENE VIII
The BARONESS, ADOLPH; *the* BARON *arrives by an alternate route.*

BARON Darn! Finally, I am here; through bushes and brush! I thought I was in the moors of Monomatapa.

BARONESS Here is our second afflicted one.

ADOLPH Oh well, my uncle, did you have a good hunt?

BARON Ah! my friend, when one has hunted the lion in the sands of Siberia, and the elephant in the forests of Calabria, what sort of pleasure do you think one finds in pursuing hares in a park?

To the tune of *De l'Epicurien*
As soon as the game flees,
And the pursuit begins
A rabbit,
A deer,
Take aim suddenly
From fear of shooting the fiercest animal.
But as the game is not large,
Very Often,

> One aims badly
> Whereas an elephant,
> BOOM,
> It is easily killed.

ADOLPH (*laughing*) And you have killed a lot of them, my uncle? (*They are seated on a bench. The Baroness, leaning against the window, spitefully listens to them.*)

BARON You are joking; you don't believe me. You are acting like my wife, but I will tell you that which I tell her: Patience, patience, I will prove all the disbelievers wrong; I will write of my travels.

BARONESS Great precaution.

ADOLPH Oh! What a pity that I have not also traveled.

BARON Like a new Alcibiades, I easily adapt to all the customs and all forms.

> To the tune of *Du vaudeville des fiancées*
> Everywhere my flexibility is admired; . . .
> Adapting people's lifestyles,
> One takes me for a Greek, in Greece;
> In Lapland, they believed I was Lappish;
> In all countries, concealing my origins,
> At every stop, Turk, Negro, Iroquois;
> Three days after my arrival in China,
> I had the air of a Chinese man.

ADOLPH Aren't you happy about having seen so many different countries, my uncle! Why have I not also roamed the world? I would have found perhaps in my steps the object that deprives me of my happiness!

BARON Ah! Of course! I am devising a means! An excellent means to prevent my wife from tormenting you in my absence.

ADOLPH What is it, my uncle?

BARON You can leave with me for America.

ADOLPH What, really, my uncle, you would take me with you?

BARON You could chose your wife yourself.

ADOLPH But my aunt will never consent to such.

BARON You know quite well that I have always done what I want. Well, I am saying this only to you: your aunt is a little touched. She is a good wife.

BARONESS Impertinent man!

ADOLPH So you think she will consent to my departure?

BARON No, she is as stubborn as a devil, but you can bypass her consent. We can leave without her knowing. I should even enjoy playing this little trick. Go prepare your things; tomorrow we leave.

BARONESS (*now in view of Adolph and the Baron; They are standing up with looks of confusion.*)

To the tune of *Bon Voyage*
Bon voyage
My dear husband,
Leave, steal away upon some faraway river;
Bon voyage,
But, between us,
My dear nephew will never leave with you.

BARON She was listening; here comes the storm already.

ADOLPH You must stand your ground. Not more than a moment ago you were so courageous.

BARON Oh! That was when she wasn't around.

BARONESS
Bon Voyage

BARONESS Listen, Adolph, I wanted Amelia to become your wife. This marriage, in terminating all the differences in our family, and in assuring you a considerable fortune, seemed suitable for you in every respect. You have now absolutely refused to marry a Frenchwoman.

BARON What a devil! He is right! He takes after his uncle. Do you know why I married you, madam? You believe, perhaps, that it was because of your spirit, your character, your virtue? Not at all. I married you because you are from Pondicherry.

BARONESS I know this, sir, I know this. Far from being irritated with the refusal of your nephew, I want to show him how dear he is to me by searching for the wife that he so desires!

BARON You will not find her.

BARONESS I have found her.

ADOLPH Could it be!

BARON You have found a savage in the department of the Seine?

BARONESS In Paris!

BARON Oh! This is more than a little difficult.

ADOLPH Oh, dear aunt, how can you thus hurt me so.

BARONESS I am not at all toying with you. She is a person of very distinguished rank in her tribe, and the peace and liberty of seas have led her to Paris, where she has garnered the admiration of everyone. She is known here as the Hottentot Venus.

ADOLPH The Venus.

BARON Hottentot. Madam Baroness, don't you think you can fool us. I will go to Paris to ascertain the truth. You take guard, I have seen the people of the world, I know all the languages.

BARONESS Very well, then, I had counted upon you to serve as a conduit between us and this marvelous woman; she has not said a word since her arrival at the château.

ADOLPH She is at the château?

BARONESS In the pavilion.

BARON (*aside*) The devil, she has me now.

ADOLPH Oh, my dear aunt! Lead me to her. My uncle, come serve as the interpreter for my love.

BARON Hottentot is precisely the only language that I do not know. That is OK; she knows perhaps some others.

BARONESS I see her coming toward us now with her governess.

BARON It appears that she is an upstanding young woman.

SCENE IX
BARON, BARONESS, ADOLPH, AMELIA *in brilliant costume of the Hottentots*, the GOVERNESS
concert music by Doche

ADOLPH
What a marvelous woman! What charms!
My spirits are moved by her appearance!

BARONESS (*aside*)
Love, the second of my projects;
I believe he is already blushing in her presence.

(*to the Baron*)

You who brave the winds and waves,
Made twenty times a tour of the world,
Look at this charming object.
What do you say of her?

BARON
I confess it,
She is really a Hottentot
Of the most beautiful sort.

TOGETHER

ADOLPH
What a marvelous woman!

BARONESS
Love

BARON
For its grace and charms,
Her nation is known throughout Europe.

ADOLPH
This candor full of charm
That heaven has put upon your face,
That smile without treachery.
In Europe such a one is never seen.

BARONESS
She is a child of nature.

ADOLPH (*approaching Amelia*)
Charming object! Oh blessed is the day
That led you to our rivers.
Do not scorn my homage
And respond to my avowal of love.
(*She laughs aloud.*)

Why does she laugh at my tenderness?

BARON
It's the custom of her country!
They always laugh at their suitors there.

ADOLPH
Everywhere is thus like Paris.

BARONESS
She cannot understand you.

ADOLPH
My uncle, make her understand
That which her beauty inspires in me.

BARON (*aside*)
Here comes the difficult part!

Reprise

TOGETHER

ADOLPH
What a marvelous woman!, etc.

BARONESS
Love, etc.,

BARON
For its grace, etc.,

BARONESS Are you satisfied, my dear Adolph?

ADOLPH Yes, my aunt! Haven't you witnessed all my gratitude? But she cannot understand me, alas; my happiness is not at all complete.

BARON I do not know Hottentot. But she has received a bit of education; she must speak Caribbean or Iroquois. These are my two favorite languages. (*To the Governess*) Well, what is her name?

GOVERNESS Liliska.

ADOLPH Such a pretty name!

BARON From where does she come?

GOVERNESS From the country of the Hottentots.

BARON I see, but what city?

GOVERNESS Sir, this is a country where there are no cities.

BARON That is correct. There are only villages, I remember.

ADOLPH But my uncle, speak to her, I beg you.

BARON Leave it to me. (*He approaches Amelia.*) Beautifula Liliskaa, Iam ata youra servicea.

(*She looks at him in astonishment.*)

Woulda youa pleasea responda toa mya nephew'sa declarationas ofa lovea.

(*Amelia gives a look of impatience.*)

She does not understand.

BARONESS What language were you speaking?

BARON It's a mixed language. All the savages of the Adriatic sea understand it; but leave it be, I am going to speak to her in Iroquois.

GOVERNESS She understands it?

BARON (*aside*) Devil! Too bad.

ADOLPH She understands it. Oh my dear uncle. I am indebted to you.

BARON (*aside*) I going to make up another language. (*Aloud*) Kaf kaof, roc mac tring koul magniac magnioc ros rif krou tring.

AMELIA (*responding to him*) Orf nec rolouf your zouf camatof ordief zic mac tring.

BARON (*embarrassed*) Yes.

ADOLPH Yes, my dear uncle, what is she saying to you?

BARON (*stupefied*) (*aside*) How in the heck do I know? I don't even know this language. (Aloud) She says that she approves of your love or something like that.

ADOLPH I was sure of it.

To the tune of *J'aime ce mot de gentillesse*
By a tender sympathy,
Our hearts have found themselves swept away,
Her sweetness and her modesty
Assure me of happy days;

To our nuptials her heart aspires,
This knot she is about to tie makes her smile,
And what she is about to say
Her eyes have already said it.

BARON I give my blessings.

ADOLPH But uncle, I want to learn this language.

BARON (*aside*) He will look a long time for its grammar.

BARONESS She has without a doubt some talent?

BARON Undoubtedly, there are some excellent boarding schools in her country.

GOVERNESS Liliska, as you were saying earlier, is a student of nature.

ADOLPH A student of nature!

To the tune of *Voulant par des œuvres*
And what! This is thus not a dream,
I am going to finally, according to my whims,
Have a young student
Who knows yet nothing.
Yes! This one thought alone gives me pleasure.
It is so rare that a husband
Finds, alas, in this country
An educational undertaking.

GOVERNESS Liliska already knows plenty of things. You yourself be the judge. (*She gives a sign. Amelia responds to her.*) She is going to sing a Hottentot song, accompanied by an instrument from her country.

BARON (*aside*) If she sings anything like she speaks.

ADOLPH She is really trying to impress me.

BARON We are listening.

AMELIA

Hottentot Song

First couplet

Ric mir voulouf izami

Crif nec romir tonoc

Mar zemu sambo semi

Zang sir colofrinoc

(*More animated*)

Allious, Allious, allious ou

Allious, nimou.

Second couplet

Zic lomen cori zoni

Rif af volin olof

Trozalouf coric ani

Crouf ragoli riolof

Allious, allious, allious, ou

Allious, nimou.

(*She dances.*)

BARON (after having repeated the refrain with her) Braviof! Braviof!

BARONESS Certainly, her voice is very agreeable.

ADOLPH I am ravished, enchanted; my dear uncle, what has she said?

BARON Shall I tell you again, I do not know this language. What she was singing is from the Hottentot they speak in the capital.

BARONESS Well, my dear Adolph, are you reluctant to give her your hand?

ADOLPH What are you saying, my aunt? Ah! I am more than ever proud of my feelings and my choice.

BARON This is the woman for you.

BARONESS I have notified a notary near here to draw up a contract. We are going to his home. Adolph, we are leaving you with Liliska.

GOVERNESS By themselves, madam?

BARON That's going to be some conversation.

BARONESS I can vouch for my nephew.

BARON And so do I.

To the tune of *L'Appetit nous reclame*
We can in this refuge
Leave them, without beating around the bush
It will be very clever
If he speaks to her of love.

ADOLPH (*aside*)
Without verbiage and without harangue
Yes, I hope to be understood.
Besides, love is a language
That one speaks in all countries.

SCENE X
AMELIA, ADOLPH

ADOLPH (*aside*) The way her eyes are looking at me. One would believe that she has something she wants to tell me and that she regrets not being able to be understood. (*Amelia approaches him while looking at him attentively.*) How she looks at me, Lovable Liliska! (*She comes closer.*)

To the tune of *De Robert le diable*
You do not have at all
That strange and savage countenance of a country
far away,
Your gaze is sweet and serene,
Grace animates your face,
Charming object, in truth
If it were not for your candor, your innocence,
I would have believed, such is your beauty,
That your fatherland was France.

(*She sits before him.*)

If you could understand me, you would know I have been awaiting you for a long time and who I have scorned for you. (*She lifts his head, holding it, and then laughs aloud*.) What a pleasing custom!

> To the tune of *Vaudeville du petit courier*
> I must tell the truth
> France, on this point, wins.
> It is too great a freedom
> Showing such delight.
> Here when a wife constantly laughs
> At the expense of her husband,
> She is at least polite enough
> Not to laugh in front of him.
> Civilization certainly has its advantages.

(*Amelia runs through the garden with a carefree, cheerful look and picks flowers to form a bouquet.*)

Adorable Liliska, I take these flowers as a token of your tenderness, and I swear at your feet an eternal love. (*He is on bended knee in order to take the bouquet; she refuses, pulling the bouquet back quickly. He rises a bit confused.*)

These savage women have some manners! (*Amelia approaches him, attempting to appease him with tenderness and gives him the flowers.*)

> To the tune of *De la Tyrolienne*
> O glorious moment!
> This is not a mistake.
> Her candor,
> Her innocence,
> Make my heart palpitate.
> My foolish vows
> Are thus fulfilled!
> Enchanting Object,
> You make me happy.
> O glorious moment! etc.

I am going to meet my aunt to hasten my bliss! Good-bye, Liliska! I take leave of you only for a moment, and I will return at your feet never again to leave. (*He leaves.*)

SCENE XI
AMELIA *alone and laughing loudly*

AMELIA You are perfectly right, my dear cousin, that there is no pleasure in making fun of you; you are so trusting and gullible. You surely deserve to be my husband. Someone is coming, I should assume my role.

SCENE XII
AMELIA, FANCHETTE

FANCHETTE (*Comes in without seeing Amelia*) I have already prepared everything for the wedding that the gentleman recommended; I alerted all the village girls to have themselves at the park entrance. The bouquets are done; the only thing missing from this marriage is the bride. (*She is near Amelia. She sees her and screams.*)

Oh, my God! (*Amelia tries to befriend her.*) This is perhaps the fiancée! (*Amelia approaches her; Fanchette moves to the other side, away from her.*) This is the savage; I am sure of it. But she looks like everybody else. (*Amelia approaches her again; Fanchette moves away again.*) She doesn't talk; are there indeed countries where women do not speak at all? (*She looks Amelia over.*) She does not appear to be mean-spirited. I should interrogate her: PSST, PSST, PSST, well! She is quite tamed.

(*Amelia approaches her laughing.*)

To the tune of *Je vais commencer à present.*
You are the savage that everyone is talking about
But perhaps you will tell me,
You can answer with a smile,
I know what that means.

And you are a savage, I see,
All in fact like me.

They say, between us,
That in your country they eat men;
But in your eyes, miss,
I read not a trace of cruelty.
And you will eat them, I can see that,
Just like me.

What a shame that you don't talk; its a great comfort that the heavens above have deprived you and not me, for in your place I would die from unhappiness.

AMELIA That would be fitting.

(*Fanchette screams and tries to save herself.*)

SCENE XIII

AMELIA, BARON, BARONESS, ADOLPH, GOVERNESS

BARONESS All of our formalities are done. The interests of our children are in order; all that remains is to sign. Never has a wedding been so quickly arranged.

BARON They will be married on the borders of the Azov sea.

ADOLPH Liliska is the wife my heart has chosen. You approve my choice. What more is there to do?

BARON He is right, this is not a marriage to a European.

ADOLPH Liliska undoubtedly approves of this marriage.

(*She looks at him without speaking.*)

BARON Is there anyone here who does not give their consent?

GOVERNESS Let's hurry up and finish.

BARONESS Let's go into this pavilion.

SCENE XIV, *Final Scene*
The entire cast, including the villagers

CHORUS
To the tune of *En revenant du village*
To dance at this marriage,
We will rush in
From everywhere.
This wedding will be I bet
The most exceptional that we will see.

CHEVALIER
Yes, it is an agreeable pairing,
The happy lovers,
Faithful, truly in love;
The beautiful and savage woman,
Certainly, there cannot be two.

CHORUS
To dance . . .

AMELIA (*aside*) It's the Chevalier! All is lost. (*She hides herself.*)

BARONESS What do all these villagers want?

ADOLPH Oh! My dear d'Ericourt, you could not have come at a better time! You will witness my happiness.

CHEVALIER Your happiness! You are darn right, I am here to bring it.

ADOLPH What do you mean?

AMELIA (*aside*) Scatterbrain!

BARON (*looking at the Chevalier's clothing*) He appears to come from China.

CHEVALIER My dear Adolph, I learned that you had made a resolution to marry only a foreigner; I approved of your decision, and I have worked to fulfill your wishes. I am introducing you to a divine woman.

ADOLPH I much appreciate your attention, my dear d'Ericourt, but I have already found her; she is before you.

CHEVALIER How?

ADOLPH By chance a charming savage, a new Atala, has arrived in Paris, and I am going to tie my fate to hers.

CHEVALIER Really, I am angry with myself for not having arrived sooner. You don't mind, I hope at any rate, seeing the beauty that I have chosen for you. She is a Venus!

BARONESS A Venus!

CHEVALIER Yes, madam, the Hottentot Venus.

EVERYONE The Hottentot Venus!

ADOLPH This is impossible.

CHEVALIER Here, look at her. (*He pulls out a large scroll of paper from his pocket.*)

CHORUS
To the tune of *De la belle au bois dormant*
What a strange thing!
And how! Two Venuses in the same place!
Without a doubt this one is an impostor;
There cannot be two.

CHEVALIER
I would easily be able to vouch for
The one who takes her name, but
It will suffice only to astonish you
With her graces and her charms.

(*He unrolls the paper and shows the portrait of the Hottentot Venus; everyone cries out in fright.*)

CHORUS
What a strange thing!
Such features until now unknown!
With such a face
She cannot be a Venus.

CHEVALIER I was sure that you would be astonished, stupefied. Hence I have made the first move with this portrait, so that the presence of the Venus in the flesh would not startle you.

ADOLPH D'Ericourt, what kind of joke is this?

BARON Do you aim to make us believe, sir, that that one there is a Hottentot, a people whose women are most renowned for their beauty?

ADOLPH (*to Amelia*) Come Liliska, come and take revenge for your countrywomen.

CHEVALIER Why I see Amelia.

EVERYONE Amelia?

ADOLPH Could it be?

BARON I saw, however, that she did not have that swarthy complexion typical of people from southern France.

ADOLPH My cousin?

AMELIA Yes, sir, your cousin whom you have refused to see, and to whom this revenge should well be allowed.

To the tune of *Du Vaudeville de Psyché*
I wanted to try
At least to cure you of your madness;
Through a cherished illusion
I was proud of myself in achieving this coup,
But one instant has destroyed my euphoria,
I see at this dark juncture,

You will continue to hate Frenchwomen,
As much as I love Frenchmen.

ADOLPH

Yes, I have sworn upon my life
I would not love a beauty
who born, in the bosom of my homeland,
would have our finesse;
But in these moments, in seeing you appear,
I cede to your kind laws.
Two times cheated, I am willing to be
Again a third.

BARON This is agreed upon, this is agreed upon? Of course. Here is a marriage that enchants me. (*To Amelia*) Embrace me my niece, I am postponing my trip on your behalf.

AMELIA You will stay with us. Together we will speak this language that you know so well.

BARON Iroquois, isn't it? You are charming. (*Aside*) What a shame she is not a savage.

BARONESS

To the tune of *de la Vallée de Barcelonnette*
Poor lovers in whom love
Has made a profound wound,
In order to be repaid in kind
Go roam the world.
Featherbrains who only cherish
Pleasure and faithlessness,
Destiny has well arranged it thus.
Do not abandon France.

CHEVALIER

Persecutors of true talent
You, whose species everywhere abounds,
Foolish innovators, vile charlatans,

Go roam the world.
You whose scattered works of art,
Demonstrate taste and science
Pride and support of the fine arts,
Do not abandon France.

FANCHETTE

Jealous husbands, for your own good
Who near a woman, brunette or blond,
Believing all, seeing nothing,
Go roam the world.
Husbands, summoned from everywhere,
Who always so trusting
Don't believe anything, seeing all
Do not abandon France.

BARON

You who with each day become more adroit,
Lie and cheat with straight faces
False Picards, shrewd Champagneans
Go roam the world.
You who will show people
Frankness and trustworthiness
Sincere Gascons, frank Normands
Do not abandon France.

ADOLPH

You who rouse infamy
In your fury at every moment
You rant against peace,
Go roam the world.
Virtuous and law-abiding friends
You who know how with valor
To die for the good of kings
Do not abandon France.

AMELIA (*to the audience*)
Censors who never laugh
Whose mean-spiritedness always rails against
Our plays and verses,
Go roam the world.
But you indulgent spectators
Who treat with benevolence
Our authors and actors,
Do not abandon France.

NOTES

Introduction: Theorizing Black Venus

1. Abélard, *Les Lettres complètes,* fifth letter, pp. 87, 89–90. My translation.

2. See Edward Ahearn, "Black Woman, White Poet." See also Jan Nederven Pieterse's mention of Baudelaire in his abbreviated discussion of Black Venus images in French literature, art, and popular culture. Pieterse also provides an abbreviated analysis of Bartmann in *White on Black,* pp. 172–87.

3. Williams and Chrisman, eds., *Colonial Discourse,* p. 194.

4. Fanon, *Black Skin, White Masks,* pp. 109–40.

5. Hayward, *French National Cinema,* pp. 119–49.

6. For more on colonial cinema, its uses and the era, see Coquery-Vidrovitch, "Le Cinéma colonial"; Nesterenko, "L'Afrique de l'autre"; Sorlin, "The Fanciful Empire"; Abel, *French Cinema;* Williams, *Republic of Images.*

7. Hayward, *French National Cinema,* pp. 119–49.

8. Dina Sherzer's "Race Matters and Matters of Race: Interracial Relationships in Colonial and Postcolonial Films," in her edited volume *Cinema, Colonialism, Postcolonialism,* is perhaps the latest exception among "French" academic feminist film critics in the United States. Boulanger's *Le Cinéma colonial* mentions the work but does not examine how representations of black women in particular functioned in colonial cinema. Baker is examined as a colonial Other, but not especially as a black female colonial Other.

9. Fanon, *Black Skin, White Masks,* pp. 110–11.

10. See Mulvey, *Visual and Other Pleasures,* p. 19.

11. Morrison, *Playing in the Dark,* p. 7.

12. Ibid., p. 7.

13. Roberts, *Whores in History,* pp. 33–54.

14. Zola, *Thérèse Raquin,* p. 93.

15. See Hayward, *French National Cinema,* p. 12.

16. Rose, *Sexuality,* p. 199.

17. See Mulvey, *Visual and Other Pleasures,* pp. 14–26.

18. Hayward, *French National Cinema,* p. 161.

19. Fanon, *Black Skin, White Masks,* p. 110.

20. Ibid., p. 116.

21. Ibid., p. 111.

22. Pierre Loti, while not on many reading lists today because of his blatant misogyny and racism, was very popular in the nineteenth and early twentieth centuries. He was elected to the Académie Française in May 1891, beating out Emile Zola.

23. In *Blank Darkness,* Christopher Miller provides a reading of Baudelaire's *La Belle Dorothée.* However, Miller's angle is not that of an explicit examination of black femininity, but rather of the meanings of blackness in the literary imagination.

24. See Charles Baudelaire, *Petits Poèmes en prose,* n. 1, pp. 116–17.

1 Writing Sex, Writing Difference

1. Gilman, *Difference and Pathology,* pp. 76–108.

2. For more on "the great chain of being" and Bartmann in the nineteenth century, see John and Jean Comaroff, *Of Revelation and Revolution,* "Africa Observed."

3. Cuvier's influence was profound. After his dissection of Bartmann, autopsies were widely performed throughout Europe and the United States on black American, Antillean, and African women. See Duchet, *Anthropologie et histoire,* for more on the opposing anthropological discourses of the eighteenth and nineteenth centuries: monogenesis and polygenesis.

4. Recounted by Bartmann at the Chancery Court in England and published in the "Law Report," *Times* (London), 29 November 1810.

5. Peter Cezar's original name was probably Pieter Kayser.

6. *Times* (London), 26 November 1810.

7. Reproduced in Edwards and Walvin, *Black Personalities,* p. 171.

8. Stott-Toole, *Circus and Allied Arts,* pp. 333–36.

9. The change in spelling from Baartman to Bartmann in the chapter follows literally and chronologically Bartmann's name change. See illustration 1 — the Baptismal certificate.

10. *Journal des dames et des modes,* 12 February 1815. See also Bernth Lindfors, " 'The Hottentot Venus' and Other African Attractions in Nine-teenth-Century England," *Australasian Drama Studies* 1 (1983): 88.

11. A copy of the manuscript is in the Bibliothèque Nationale in Paris.

12. Frédéric Cuvier and Etienne Geoffroy St.-Hilaire, *Histoire naturelle des mammifères* (Paris, 1824). All translations of excerpts are mine and from this edition of the text.

13. Jay, *Downcast Eyes,* p. 8.

14. The text on Bartmann by Georges Cuvier, besides appearing in *His-toire naturelle de mammifères,* can also be found under the title, "Extraits d'observation faites sur le cadavre d'une femme connue à Paris et à Lon-dres sous le nom de Vénus Hottentote," in *Discours sur les révolutions du globe* (Paris: Passard, 1864), pp. 211–22. It is from this reprinted and more readily available version of the text in the United States that this and the following excerpts are taken. All translations are mine.

15. In addition to Cuvier's comparisons, see nineteenth-century natu-ralist Virey's *Histoire naturelle du genre humain* and his article in the *Dic-tionnaire des sciences médicales* 35 (1819): 398–403. Virey's discussion of blacks is also included in Guenebault's *Natural History of the Negro Race.*

16. In his closing arguments on Bartmann and black inferiority, Cuvier reflects upon the greatness of the ancient race of Egyptians and concludes that they were definitely white in intellect (221).

17. See Cuvier, *Le Règne animal,* p. 95.

18. See Jordonova, *Sexual Visions,* p. 29.

19. Cited in Jordonova, *Sexual Visions,* p. 29.

20. Jordonova, *Sexual Visions,* pp. 99–100.

21. There is some confusion as to her date of death. Records at the museum list the date as January 1, 1816, while Cuvier maintains it was December 29, 1815.

22. Both Le Vaillant and Barrow are cited in Avalon, "Sarah, La Venus hottentote." Le Vaillant says in his *Voyage dans l'intérieur de l'Afrique* (1790) that he had only seen four women and one young girl in this ridiculous state ("dans cet état ridicule").

23. "Labial hypertrophy" is not a racially specific characteristic. It has been found in Africans, African Americans, Asians, and European and Euro-American women. See the journal *Woman: An Historical Gynaeco-logical and Anthropological Compendium* as well as a host of articles in contemporary medical literature, although most are shot through with racist-sexist discourse.

24. Gilman, *Difference and Pathology,* pp. 76–108.

2 Representing Sarah — Same Difference or No Difference at All?

1. Jean Avalon, "Sarah, La Vénus Hottentote," *L'Æsculape* 16 (1926): 281. Translations from this work are mine. See also the collection of Verneau's papers at the Museum of Man.

2. Marie-Emmanuel-Guillaume-Marguerite Théaulon, Armand Dartois, and Brasier, *La Vénus hottentote, ou haine aux Françaises* (Paris: Martinet, 1814). The translation of the entire vaudeville is in the appendix. All translations in this chapter are mine and from this edition of text.

3. See Reinelt and Roach, *Critical Theory and Performance*, p. 13. See also Jameson, *The Political Unconscious*.

4. Freud, *Jokes*, pp. 96–97.

5. Ibid., p. 103. The hidden cultural implications of comedic sitcoms are evident everywhere in American television. One need only tune in to old segments of *Good Times, The Jeffersons,* and *Amos and Andy* to see the ways that comedy operates to reinforce cultural stereotypes of blacks. American minstrel shows, where white men made up in blackface played out their fantasies of black men, implicating many a laughing third party in the process, represent another example of the insidious nature and cultural implications of jokes and comedies.

6. Foster, *Recodings*, p. 166.

7. French men flocked to see Bartmann from 11:00 A.M. to 10:00 P.M. at rue St. Honoré. She was displayed nude except for an "apron" that covered her genitalia. This apron became a highly eroticized article of clothing. According to Corbin's *Women for Hire*, prostitutes adopted the dress and attitudes of maids (*les bonnes, femmes de chambre*) during the nineteenth century. And while I agree with Corbin's assertion that French male clients fetishized the apron because of its resemblance to underwear, I maintain in chapter 5 that it was Bartmann's apron that prompted this fetishization. For more on Bartmann's popularity, see Avalon, "Sarah, La Vénus Hottentote," pp. 281–88. See also chapter 5 in this study.

8. See Gilman, *Difference and Pathology*, pp. 76–108.

9. Brewer, "Diderot," p. 54.

10. Boskin, *Sambo*, p. 14. Boskins discusses Sambo's dissemination throughout Europe and America from England.

11. Sung to the tune of *De la Belle au bois dormant*.

12. Avalon, "Sarah, La Venus Hottentote," p. 281.

13. *La Fille aux yeux d'or* (*The Girl with the Golden Eyes*) is discussed

in chapter 3. A novel replete with the themes of incest, bisexuality, and lesbianism, it is situated in Paris. The key characters are Henri, his estranged half-sister, Mariquita, and an exotic slave woman, Paquita. The slave woman is involved in an affair with the estranged siblings. Paquita is the ideal woman for Henri, but she is also the property of Mariquita. The slave woman is murdered at the end by Mariquita because of the former's sexual treason. The denouement is marked by the siblings' scene of mutual recognition ("Is Lord Dudley your father?") and incestuous (sexual) attraction. The two reunited siblings kiss as the slave woman expires in her own blood. Difference is violently purged.

3 "The Other Woman"

1. Freud, *New Introductory Lectures,* p. 102.
2. Irigaray, *Speculum de l'autre femme,* p. 26.
3. Kadish, "Hybrids," p. 270. According to Kadish, hybrids are heterogeneous groupings in one body (i.e., French and English, male and female).
4. Balzac, *La Duchesse de Langeais suivi de La Fille aux yeux d'or* (Paris: Le Livre de Poche, 1958). All translations of excerpts are mine and from this edition of the text.
5. See Miller's seminal analysis of Baudelaire's conception of creolity in *Blank Darkness.* Miller cites Baudelaire's essay on Leconte de Lisle, in which Baudelaire writes of the Creole poet in terms of "la langueur, la gentillesse, une faculté naturelle d'imitation qu'ils partagent d'ailleurs avec les nègres. . . ." Vivacity is the antonym of languor, just as black and white are diametrically opposed in the nineteenth-century discourse on race. If languidness is a characteristic of the black, then vivacity is conversely a characteristic of the white. The Creole is the embodiment of these racial and linguistic opposites.
6. Hoffman, *Le Nègre romantique,* p. 248.
7. Under the rubric *négresse,* Flaubert writes in his *Dictionnaire des idées reçues,* p. 61: "Elles sont plus volupteuses que les blanches." In his *Histoire naturelle,* Virey describes the négresse as "très ardente en amour" and "elles portent la volupté jusqu'à des lascivetés ignorées dans nos climats" (150). The mulâtresse with black blood will share some of the négresse's characteristics.
8. JanMohamed, "Manichean Allegory," p. 85. JanMohamed's analysis borrows heavily from Frantz Fanon.

9. Baudelaire, *Œuvres complètes*, vol. 1, p. 687. The citation in its entirety reads, "Le dandy doit aspirer à être sublime sans interruption, il doit vivre et dormir devant un miroir."

10. See Gobineau's *Essai sur l'inégalité des races humaines*.

11. Gilman notes in *Difference and Pathology* that the black servant in visual arts represents the sexualization of the society in which he or she is found. This observation could equally be made of literary representations of blacks (pp. 76–79). See also Morrison, *Playing the Dark*.

12. See Felman's "Re-reading Femininity." According to Felman, Mariquita means homosexual man in Spanish.

13. See Felman's interpretation in "Re-reading Femininity," pp. 19–44.

14. Balzac, *Cousin Bette, Pierre Grassou, The Girl with the Golden Eyes*, trans. George Ives et al., p. 423.

15. JanMohamed, "Manichean Allegory," p. 83.

16. Kadish, "Hybrids," p. 276.

17. One could argue plausibly that because of the utter sadness expressed by the marquise at the novella's end and Henri's description of Paquita as an ideal woman that Paquita represents more than an exchangeable-disposable object. However, this argument is flawed when one considers that despite the marquise's sadness, when asked about the police, she says that no one would avenge Paquita's murder except Christemio, whom she has also murdered. Hence Paquita's disposability. Her exchangeability is glaringly apparent in the exchange of gold for her murder. De Marsay's idyllic characterizations of the slave woman are perverse at best. Henri is attracted to Paquita's *differentness*, which he describes in sexually racialized language. She is a sexual *object*, an abyss of pleasures. Paquita represents a prototype, "that feminine variety" which one "rarely sees in France," but does see in other countries. She is unique because she has been imported to a place—France—where Other women are rarely encountered. And just as easily as de Marsay dreams of her, so readily does he want to murder her, and then he quickly forgets her after she is murdered.

18. Cited from Brooks, *Body Work*, p. 84. See also Crépet, *Pensées, Sujets, Fragments*, p. 45.

19. Brooks, *Body Work*, p. 84.

4 *Ourika, L'Africaine*

1. See Roger Mercer, *L'Afrique noire,* pp. 162–65.

2. Ibid., p. 165. My translation.

3. Doris Kadish, "Translation of Duras," in *Translating Slavery: Gender and Race in French, Women's Writing, 1783–1823,* ed. Doris Kadish and Françoise Massardier-Kenney (Kent, OH: Kent State University Press, 1994). All translations of Duras's *Ourika* are from this essay.

4. Fanon, *Black Skin, White Masks,* p. 64.

5. Ibid., p. 65.

6. Gaspard de Pons *Ourika, l'Africaine,* in *Inspirations poètiques* (Paris: Urbain Canel, 1825). All translations of excerpts are mine (they are loose content-based translations rather than strivings for poetic perfection) and from this edition of the text.

7. Claire de Duras's Ourika is fraught with guilt over the massacres in Saint Domingue. She tells the reader, "The Saint Domingue massacres caused me a new, excruciating pain: Until then, I had been distressed to belong to a proscribed race; now I was ashamed of belonging to a race of barbarians and murderers" (203).

8. Montesquieu, *Spirit of the Laws,* p. 250.

9. Girardin, *Œuvres complètes,* Vol. 1, pp. 233–35.

10. Abdul JanMohamed, "The Manichean Allegory," in *Race, Writing, and Difference,* p. 86.

11. The black-white woman is present in several works, such as Abbé Prévost's *Voyage de Capitaine Ladé,* La Fontaine's *Les Amours de Psiché and de Cupidon,* and Loti's *Le Roman d'un spahi* (see chap. 8).

12. bell hooks, *Black Looks,* p. 26.

13. See Abbeele, "Utopian Sexuality," pp. 50–51.

14. Hoffman, *Le Nègre romantique,* p. 195.

15. Ourika's and Paquita's deaths are strikingly similar. Both are *poignardée.*

5 Black Is the Difference

1. Baudelaire, *Les Fleurs du mal,* pp. 37, 39.

2. See Clark, "Elements of Black Exoticism," p. 65. See also Miller, *Blank Darkness,* pp. 69–138.

3. *Baudelaire, Petits Poèmes en prose: Le Spleen de Paris* (Paris: Classique Garnier, 1980). All translations of excerpts are mine and from this edition of the text.

4. See Miller, *Blank Darkness*, p. 121. Miller dates the letter February 6, 1834. However, I have looked at several collections of Baudelaire's letters to his mother and did not discover this letter. This does not change the fact that Le Vaillant is the poet's great-uncle (through marriage) and the fact that the work does contain this photo. Moreover, Françoise Lionnet critiques Miller's shortsightedness on the origins of the word "Cafrine." According to Lionnet in *Autobiographical Voices*, p. 28, n. 42: "The term is a creole neologism, widely used in the islands of Réunion and Mauritius where Baudelaire spent time in 1841." For a more developed discussion of these issues, see Lionnet's forthcoming article, "Reframing Baudelaire," in *Diacritics*. For our purposes, we shall stick to Le Vaillant's *Voyage* as the initial source for Baudelaire's use of "cafrine," a derivative/neologism from "Femme caffre."

5. In *Blank Darkness*, Miller notes that Baudelaire creates an "imaginary geography," a conflation of orientalism and africanism, in his references to Dorothée as a member of "la race noire des côtes orientales." Studies by Le Vaillant, Cuvier, and a great many other natural historians and ethnographers consistently remark on the admixture the "Hottentots" appear to possess: part Negro, part "Mongoloid" (large cheekbones, horizontal eyes, and flatness of face). We find this same association of Asia and Africa in the poem "La Chevelure" from *Les Fleurs du mal*.

6. Corbin, *Les Filles de noce*, p. 305. My translation.

7. Ibid., pp. 275–314.

8. Cuvier and St. Hilaire, *Histoire naturelle*, p. 4.

9. See chap. 1, "Writing Sex, Writing Difference: Creating the Master Text on the Hottentot Venus." See also Gilman, *Difference and Pathology*, pp. 76–108.

10. It is interesting to note Pieterse's observation in *White on Black* that in twentieth-century advertising black women are disproportionately featured as domestic servants (183). This is partly owing to the fact that migrating black Antillean and African women were marginalized into domestic service, one of the only viable sources of employment in France. This was also the trend in the United States as late as the 1980s —so much so, that domestic work became popularly known as "black women's work." And it is within these domestic spaces, in proximity to white males, that sexual violence has historically taken place. See Davis,

Women, Race, and Class; Collins, *Black Feminist Thought;* and James, "Ella Baker."

11. Fanon, *Wretched of the Earth,* p. 250.

12. Fanon, *Black Skin, White Masks,* p. 98.

13. Miller, *Blank Darkness,* p. 120.

14. Lindsey, "The Black Woman," p. 88.

6 Desirous and Dangerous Imaginations

1. Gilman, *Difference and Pathology,* pp. 5, 99.

2. Alexandre Parent-Duchâtelet, *La Prostitution à Paris,* pp. 70–71. All translations are mine.

3. Debrunner, *Presence to Prestige,* p. 102.

4. Henriques, *Prostitution,* p. 132.

5. See Reich, *Compulsory Sex Morality,* p. 164.

6. Corbin, *Les Filles de noces,* p. 16. Corbin analyzes Parent-Duchâtelet's views on the prostitute.

7. Corbin, *Les Filles de noces,* pp. 275–90.

8. Parent-Duchâtelet, *La Prostitution à Paris,* pp. 135–36.

9. Ibid., p. 87.

10. Ibid., pp. 128–29.

11. Ibid., pp. 87–94. Parent-Duchâtelet also suggests that vanity and laziness lead to prostitution.

12. See Hoffman's discussion of the mulâtresse in *Le Nègre romantique,* p. 248.

13. Emile Zola, *Thérèse Raquin* (Paris: Garnier-Flammarion, 1970), p. 61. After he was besieged by criticism, Zola added a preface to the novel in which he referred to several harsh commentaries on himself and the novel. All translations of excerpts are mine and from this edition of the text.

14. Originally published in *Le Figaro,* 23 January 1868; see also *Thérèse Raquin,* p. 40.

15. Originally published in *Le Figaro,* 31 January 1868; see also *Thérèse Raquin,* pp. 44–48.

16. See Zola, *Œuvres complètes,* pp. 272–76. Mitterand also notes that the source for *Un mariage d'amour* was a story published in *Le Figaro* in 1866 entitled "La Vénus Gordes" by Adolphe Belot and Ernest Daudet.

17. As Brooks notes in *Body Work,* Zola's novels typically equate female

sexuality with the lower classes (see pp. 123–61). In *Thérèse Raquin* this equation is extended to a discourse on race.

18. See McClendon, "Red on Gray," pp. 304–16. Also Kaminskas, "*Thérèse Raquin*," pp. 23–31.

19. In the new preface to the English language edition of *Women for Hire*, p. xiv, Corbin discusses the likening of the prostitute to spontaneous, animal-like sexuality. In *Thérèse Raquin*, there is also a cat. Zola likens Thérèse to a feline and a wild animal. See also Torgovnick's *Gone Primitive*, pp. 99–102, for a discussion of Manet's painting and the "pussy" cat, and Bernheimer, *Figures of Ill Repute*.

20. Gilman, *Difference and Pathology*, pp. 76–79. See Torgovnick, *Gone Primitive*, pp. 99–104.

21. Zola, "Edouard Manet," pp. 160–61. My translation.

22. Note again the similarities between Zola's mixed-race Thérèse and Balzac's Creole Paquita. Both authors describe the felinity of each personage and movements that betray slumbering passion.

23. Balzac uses the low forehead as a sign of Christemio's childlike irrationality in *La Fille aux yeux d'or*. Gobineau and Virey also use physiognomy to read intellectual capacity and national character.

24. Zola, *Thérèse Raquin*, preface to the second edition, p. 60.

25. Parent-Duchâtelet, *La Prostitution à Paris*, p. 95.

7 Can a White Man Love a Black Woman?

1. Fanon, *Black Skin, White Masks*, p. 42.

2. Guy de Maupassant, *Contes et nouvelles*, vol. 2 (Paris: Gallimard, 1979), pp. 1086–94. All translations of excerpts are mine and from this edition of the text.

3. See Todorov, *On Human Diversity*, p. 265. Todorov discusses the fact that it is the tendency of the exoticist to "cherish that which is remote from us."

4. Bhabha, "Of Mimicry and Man," pp. 125–33.

5. Fanon, *Black Skin, White Masks*, p. 8.

8 Bamboulas, Bacchanals, and Dark Veils

1. See Szyliowicz, *Loti and the Oriental Woman*. According to Szyliowicz, the orientalist works are comprised of *Le Mariage de Loti*, *Aziyadé*,

La Troisième Jeunesse de Mme. Prune, Le Roman d'un spahi, Fleurs d'ennui, Fantôme d'orient, and *Les Désenchantées.*

2. The reader will notice that in other places in this book (see chap. 1) where the word *nègre* appears, I have used *Negro* in its place. In the case of Georges Cuvier, I granted his usage of the word to denote the racial category *Negro,* in the spirit of his scientific inquiry, despite the tract's racist underpinnings. However, since Loti uses *nègre* in so many places to emphasize a sort of degraded difference, *nigger* seemed the closest English/American pejorative equivalent.

3. Pierre Loti, *Le Roman d'un spahi* (Paris: Calmann-Lévy, 1881). All translations of excerpts are mine and from this edition of the text.

4. Fanon, *Black Skin, White Masks,* p. 177.

5. Ibid., p. 47.

6. Fanoudh-Seifer, *Le Mythe du nègre,* p. 60.

7. It is interesting to note that Loti categorizes Cora as a mulattress, when she is in fact the granddaughter, *"petite-fille,"* of a slave, not the daughter. Hence she is a woman of color, but not a mulattress. He is merely falling back then on the nineteenth-century *idea* of the mulattress and the Creole woman as well, for literary effect.

9 Cinematic Venus in the Africanist Orient

1. Flanner, *Paris Was Yesterday,* p. xx.

2. Stovall, *Paris Noir,* p. 33.

3. Buss, *The French through Their Films,* pp. 33–34.

4. Cited in Hammond and O'Connor, *Josephine Baker,* p. 20.

5. Kessler, *In the Twenties,* p. 279.

6. Buss, *The French through Their Films,* p. 13.

7. Ibid., p. 21.

8. See Marchel, *Film Study,* p. 435.

9. Sorlin, "The Fanciful Empire," pp. 135–51.

10. Ibid., p. 136.

11. Boulanger, *Le Cinéma colonial,* p. 5.

12. Sorlin, "The Fanciful Empire," pp. 150–51.

13. Marchel, *Film Study,* p. 456.

14. Ungar, "Split Screens," p. 37.

15. Boulanger, *Le Cinéma colonial,* p. 91.

16. All translations of the film dialogue are mine.

17. Fanon, *Black Skin, White Masks,* p. 129.

18. Hayward, *French National Cinema,* p. 161.

19. Fanon, *Black Skin, White Masks,* p. 129.

Epilogue

1. hooks, *Black Looks,* p. 77.

2. Cixous, "Laugh of the Medusa," p. 250.

3. Mordecai and Wilson, *Her True True Name,* p. x.

4. See Lara, *Histoire de la Guadeloupe,* and André Schwarz-Bart's historic novel, *La Mulâtresse Solitude.* André Schwarz-Bart is the husband of Guadeloupean novelist Simone Schwarz-Bart. Free of exoticisms, his novel has a very rich and vividly descriptive narrative.

5. Not all writings by Francophone women are inherently oppositional. Some merely reinscribe ideas about black women rather than subverting dominant economies of representation. See, for instance, Capécia's *La Négresse blanche.*

6. Marie Chauvet, *Amour, colère, folie* (Paris: Gallimard, 1968). All translations of excerpts are mine.

7. Cited in Zimra, "Haitian Literature," p. 84.

8. Ibid., pp. 77–93.

9. Myriam Warner-Vieyra, *Juletane* (Paris: Présence Africaine, 1982). All translations of excerpts are mine.

WORKS CITED

Abbeele, Georges Van Den. "Utopian Sexuality and Its Discontents: Exoticism and Colonialism in the *Supplément au Voyage de Bougainville*." *Esprit Créateur* 24 (1984): 43–52.

Abel, Richard. *French Cinema: The First Wave, 1915–1929*. Princeton: Princeton University Press, 1984.

Abélard, Peter. *Lettres complètes d'Abélard et d'Héloïse*. Paris: Garnier Frères, 1870.

Ahearn, Edward. "Black Woman, White Poet: Exile and Exploitation in Jeanne Duval Poems." *French Review* 51, no. 2 (December 1977): 212–20.

Alexander, Elizabeth. *The Venus Hottentot*. Charlottesville: University Press of Virginia, 1990.

Avalon, Jean. "Sarah, La Venus hottentote." *L'Æsculupe* 16 (1926): 281–88.

Balzac, Honoré de. *Cousin Bette, Pierre Grassou, The Girl with the Golden Eyes*. Translated by George Ives et al. Philadelphia: George Barrie & Son, 1896.

———. *La Duchesse de Langeais suivi de La Fille aux yeux d'or*. Paris: Le Livre de Poche, 1958.

Barrow, John. *An Account of Travels into the Interior of South Africa in the Years 1797–1798*. London: Cadell J. Davies, 1801–4.

Baudelaire, Charles. *Curiosités esthètiques: L'Art romantique*. Paris: Garnier Frères, 1962.

———. *Les Fleurs du mal*. Paris: Librairie Générale Française, 1972.

———. *Œuvres complètes*. Paris: Gallimard, 1975.

———. *Petits Poèmes en prose: Le Spleen de Paris*. Edited by Henri Lemaître. Paris: Classique Garnier, 1980.

Bernheimer, Charles. *Figures of Ill Repute: Representing Prostitution in Nineteenth-Century France*. Cambridge: Harvard University Press, 1989.

Bhabha, Homi K. "Of Mimicry and Man: The Ambivalence of Colonial Discourse." *October* 28 (spring 1984): 125–33.

Boskin, Joseph. *Sambo: The Rise and Demise of an American Jester.* Oxford: Oxford University Press, 1986.

Bougainville, Louis Antoine de. *Voyage autour du monde.* Paris: Maspero, 1980.

Boulanger, Pierre. *Le Cinéma colonial de "l'Atlantide" à "Lawrence d'Arabie."* Paris: Seghers, 1975.

Brewer, Daniel. "Diderot and the Image of the Other (Woman)." *Esprit Créateur* 24 (spring 1984): 53–65.

Brooks, Peter. *Body Work: Objects of Desire in Modern Narrative.* Cambridge: Harvard University Press, 1993.

Buffon, Georges Louis Leclerc de. *De l'homme.* Paris: Vialetay, 1971.

Buss, Robin. *The French through Their Films.* New York: Ungar, 1988.

Capécia, Mayotte. *La Négresse blanche.* Paris: Corrêa, 1950.

Chamoiseau, Patrick, and Raphael Confiant. *Lettres créoles: Tracées antillaises et continentales de la littérature, 1635–1975.* Paris: Hatier, 1991.

Chauvet, Marie. *Amour, colère, folie.* Paris: Gallimard, 1968.

Cixous, Hélène. "The Laugh of the Medusa." In *New French Feminisms.* Edited by Elaine Marks and Isabelle Courtivron. Brighton, England: Harvester, 1980.

Clark, Beatrice Smith. "Elements of Black Exoticism in the 'Jeane Duval' Poems of *Les Fleurs du mal.*" *CLA Journal* 14, no. 1 (September 1970): 63–65.

Collins, Patricia. *Black Feminist Thought.* New York: Routledge, 1990.

Comaroff, John, and Jean Comaroff. *Of Revelation and Revolution: Christianity, Colonialism, and Consciousness in South Africa.* Chicago: University of Chicago Press, 1991.

Condé, Maryse. *La Parole des femmes: Essai sur romancières des Antilles de langue française.* Paris: L'harmattan, 1993.

Coquery-Vidrovitch, Catherine. "Le Cinéma colonial." In *Histoire de la France coloniale, 1914–1990.* Edited by Jacques Thobie, Gilbert Meynier, Catherine Coquery-Vidrovitch, and Charles-Robert Ageron. Paris: Armand Colin, 1990.

Corbin, Alain. *Les Filles de noce: Misère sexuelle et prostitution aux dixneuvième et vingtième siècles.* Paris: Aubier Montaigne, 1978.

———. *Women for Hire: Prostitution and Sexuality in France after 1850.* Translated by Alan Sheridan. Cambridge: Harvard University Press, 1990.

Crépet, Jacques, ed. *Pensées, Sujets, Fragments.* Paris: Blaizot, 1910.

Cuvier, Frédéric, and St. Hilaire, Geoffroy. *Histoire naturelle des mammifères.* Paris: A. Belin, 1824–27.

Cuvier, Georges. *Le Règne animal.* Paris: Chez Deterville, 1817.

Cuvier, Georges, et al. *Discours sur les révolutions du globe.* Paris: Passard, 1864.

Davis, Angela. *Women, Race, and Class.* New York: Vintage, 1983.

Debrunner, Hans Werner. *Presence to Prestige: A History of Africans in Europe before 1918.* Switzerland: Baster Afrika Bibliographen, 1979.

Diderot, Denis. *Supplément au voyage de Bougainville, Pensées philosophiques, Lettres sur les aveugles.* Paris: Garnier-Flammarion, 1972.

Duchet, Michèle. *Anthropologie et histoire au siècle des lumières: Buffon, Voltaire, Rousseau, Helvétius, Diderot.* Paris: Librairie François Maspero, 1971.

Duras, Claire de. *Ourika.* Exeter, U.K.: University of Exeter Press, 1993.

Edwards, Paul, and James Walvin. *Black Personalities in the Era of the Slave Trade.* Baton Rouge: Louisiana State University Press, 1983.

Fanon, Frantz. *The Wretched of the Earth.* Translated by Constance Farrington. New York: Grove Press, 1963.

———. *Black Skin, White Masks.* Translated by Charles Lamm Markmann. New York: Grove Press, 1967.

Fanoudh-Seifer, Léon. *Le Mythe du nègre et de l'Afrique noire dans la littérature française de 1800 à la deuxième guerre mondiale.* Paris: Librairie C. Klincksieck, 1968.

Felman, Shoshana. "Re-reading Femininity." *Yale French Studies* 62 (1981): 19–44.

Flanner, Janet. *Paris Was Yesterday.* New York: Viking, 1972.

Flaubert, Gustave. *Dictionnaire des idées reçues.* Paris: Aubier, 1951.

Foster, Hal. *Recodings: Art, Spectacle, Cultural Politics.* Seattle: Bay Press, 1985.

Freud, Sigmund. *Jokes and Their Relation to the Unconscious.* Translated by James Strachey. New York: W. W. Norton, 1963.

———. *New Introductory Lectures on Psychoanalysis.* Translated by James Strachey. New York: W. W. Norton, 1965.

Gilman, Sander. *Difference and Pathology: Stereotypes of Sexuality, Race and Madness.* Ithaca, N.Y.: Cornell University Press, 1985.

Girardin, Emile de. *Œuvres complètes.* Paris: Henri Plan, 1861.

Gobineau, Jean Arthur de. *Essai sur l'inégalité des races humaines.* Paris: Pierre Belfond, 1967.

Guenebault, J. H. *Natural History of the Negro Race.* Charleston, S.C.: D. J. Dowling, 1837.

Hammond, Bryan, and Patrick O'Connor. *Josephine Baker.* London: Cape, 1988.

Hayward, Susan. *French National Cinema.* New York: London Routledge, 1993.

Henriques, Fernando. *Prostitution in Europe and the Americas.* New York: Citadel Press, 1963.

Hoffman, Léon-François. *Le Nègre romantique: Personnage littéraire et obsession collective.* Paris: Payot, 1973.

hooks, bell. *Black Looks: Race and Representation.* Boston: South End Press, 1992.

Irigaray, Luce. *Speculum de l'autre femme.* Paris: Editions de Minuit, 1974.

————. *Ce sexe qui n'en est pas un.* Paris: Editions de Minuit, 1977.

James, Joy. "Ella Baker, Black Women's Work and Activist-Intellectual." In *Spoils of War: Women of Color, Cultures and Revolutions.* Edited by T. Sharpley-Whiting and Renée T. White. Lanham, Md.: Rowman and Littlefield, 1997.

Jameson, Russell. *Montesquieu et L'Esclavage.* New York: Lenox Hill, 1911.

JanMohamed, Abdul. "The Economy of the Manichean Allegory: The Function of Racial Difference in Colonialist Literature." In *Race, Writing, and Difference.* Edited by Henry Louis Gates Jr. Chicago: University of Chicago Press, 1986.

Jay, Martin. *Downcast Eyes: The Denigration of Vision in Twentieth-Century French Thought.* Berkeley: University of California Press, 1993.

Jordonova, Ludmilla. *Sexual Visions: Images of Gender in Science and Medicine between the Eighteenth and Twentieth Centuries.* Madison: University of Wisconsin Press, 1989.

Kadish, Doris. "Hybrids in Balzac's *La Fille aux yeux d'or.*" *Nineteenth-Century French Studies* 16 (1988): 270–78.

Kadish, Doris, and Massardier-Kenney, Françoise, eds. *Translating Slavery: Gender and Race in French Women's Writing, 1783–1823.* Kent, Ohio: Kent State University Press, 1994.

Kaminskas, Jurate. "*Thérèse Raquin:* Les Couleurs de l'abîme." *Les Cahiers Naturalistes* 58 (1985): 23–31.

Kessler, Harry. *In the Twenties: The Diary of Harry Kessler.* New York: Holt, Rinehart & Winston, 1971.

Kirby, Percival. "More on the Hottentot Venus." *Africana Notes and News* 10 (1935): 124–34.

————. "The Hottentot Venus." *Africana Notes and News* 6 (1949): 55–62.

————. "La Vénus hottentote en Angleterre." *L'Æsculupe* (January 1952): 14–21.

La Fontaine, Jean de. *Œuvres complètes.* Paris: Pagnerre, 1689.

Lara, Oruno. *Histoire de la Guadeloupe 1492-1920*. Paris: Nouvelle Librairie Universelle, 1923.

Le Vaillant, François. *Voyage dans l'intérieur de l'Afrique*. Paris: De l'imprimerie de Crapelet, 1790.

Lindfors, Bernth. " 'The Hottentot Venus' and other African Attractions in Nineteenth-Century England." *Australasian Drama Studies* 1 (1983): 83–104.

Lindsey, Kay. "The Black Woman as Woman." In *The Black Woman: An Anthology*. Edited by Toni Cade Bambara. New York: Mentor, 1970.

Lionnet, Françoise. *Autobiographical Voices: Race, Gender, and Self-Portraiture*. Ithaca, N.Y.: Cornell University Press, 1989.

———. "Reframing Baudelaire: Literary History, Biography, and Vernacular Language." *Diacritics*. Forthcoming.

Loti, Pierre. *Le Roman d'un spahi*. Paris: Calmann-Lévy, 1881.

Marchel, Frank. *Film Study*. London: Associated University Press, 1990.

Maupassant, Guy de. *Contes et nouvelles*. Vol. 2. Paris: Editions Gallimard, 1979.

McClendon, Wendell. "Red on Gray: *Thérèse Raquin*." *Nineteenth-Century French Studies* 19, no. 2 (winter 1991): 304–16.

Mercer, Roger. *L'Afrique noire dans la littérature française: Les Premières Images (dix-septième et dix-huitième siècles)*. Dakar: Université de Dakar, 1962.

Miller, Christopher. *Blank Darkness: Africanist Discourse in French*. Chicago: University of Chicago Press, 1985.

Montesquieu. *Spirit of the Laws*. Cambridge: Cambridge University Press, 1989.

Mordecai, Pamela, and Betty Wilson, eds. *Her True True Name: An Anthology of Women's Writings from the Caribbean*. Portsmouth, N.H.: Heinemann, 1990.

Morrison, Toni. *Playing in the Dark: Whiteness and the Literary Imagination*. New York: Vintage Books, 1993.

Mulvey, Laura. *Visual and Other Pleasures*. Bloomington: Indiana University Press, 1989.

Nesterenko, Geneviève. "L'Afrique de l'autre." In *Génériques des années 30*. Edited by Michèle Lagny, Marie-Claire Ropars, and Pierre Sorlin. Paris: Presse Universitaire de Vincennes, 1986.

Parent-Duchâtelet, Alexandre. *La Prostitution à Paris au dix-neuvième siècle*. Edited by Alain Corbin. Paris: Editions Seuil, 1981.

Pieterse, Jan Nederven. *White on Black: Images of Africa and Blacks in Western Popular Culture*. New Haven: Yale University Press, 1992.

Pons, Gaspard de. *Ourika l'Africaine*. In *Inspirations poètiques*. Paris: Urbain Canel, 1825.

Reich, Wilhelm. *Invasion of Compulsory Sex Morality*. New York: Farrar, Straus and Giroux, 1971.

Reinelt, Janelle, and Roach, Joseph. *Critical Theory and Performance*. Ann Arbor: University of Michigan Press, 1992.

Roberts, Nickie. *Whores in History*. London: Grafton, 1992.

Rose, Jacqueline. *Sexuality and the Field of Vision*. London: Verso, 1986.

Schwarz-Bart, André. *La Mulâtresse Solitude*. Paris: Editions du Seuil, 1972.

Schwarz-Bart, Simone. *Pluie et vent sur Telumée Miracle*. Paris: Editions du Seuil, 1972.

Sharpley-Whiting, T. Denean, and Renée T. White, eds. *Spoils of War: Women of Color, Cultures, and Revolutions*. Lanham, Md.: Rowman & Littlefield, 1997.

Sherzer, Dina, ed. *Cinema, Colonialism, Postcolonialism: Perspectives from the French and Francophone Worlds*. Austin: University of Texas Press, 1996.

Sorlin, Pierre. "The Fanciful Empire: French Feature Films and the Colonies in the 1930s." *French Cultural Studies* 2, no. 5 (June 1991): 135–51.

Stott-Toole, R. *Circus and Allied Arts: A World Bibliography 1500–1962*. Derby, U.K.: Harpur, 1962.

Stovall, Tyler. *Paris Noir: African Americans in the City of Light*. New York: Houghton Mifflin, 1996.

Szyliowicz, Irene. *Pierre Loti and the Oriental Woman*. New York: St. Martin's Press, 1988.

Théalon, Marie-Emmanuel-Guillaume-Marguerite, Armand Dartois, and Brasier. *La Vénus hottentote, ou haine aux Françaises*. Paris: Chez Martinet, 1814.

Todorov, Tzetvan. *On Human Diversity: Nationalism, Racism, and Exoticism in French Thought*. Cambridge: Harvard University Press, 1993.

Torgovnick, Marianna. *Gone Primitive: Savage Intellects, Modern Lives*. Chicago: University of Chicago Press, 1990.

Ungar, Steven. "Split Screens: *Maison de Maltais* as Text and Document." In *Cinema, Colonialism, Postcolonialism: Perspectives from the French and Francophone Worlds*. Edited by Dina Sherzer. Austin: University of Texas Press, 1996.

Virey, Julien-Joseph. *Histoire naturelle du genre humain*. 1st ed. Paris: Crochard, 1801.

Warner-Vieyra, Myriam. *Juletane*. Paris: Présence Africaine, 1982.

Williams, Alan. *Republic of Images: A History of French Filmmaking.* Cambridge: Harvard University Press, 1992.

Williams, Patrick, and Laura Chrisman, eds. *Colonial Discourse and Post-colonial Theory.* New York: Columbia University Press, 1994.

Zimra, Clarisse. "Haitian Literature after Duvalier: An Interview with Yanick Lahens." *Callaloo* 16, no. 1 (winter 1993): 77–93.

Zola, Emile. *Thérèse Raquin.* Paris: Garnier-Flammarion, 1970.

———. *Nana.* Paris: Livres Poches, 1984.

———. *Œuvres complètes.* Edited by Henri Mitterand. Paris: Cercle du livre précieux, 1986.

———. "Edouard Manet, étude biographique et critique." In *Ecrits sur l'art.* Paris: Gallimard, 1991.

INDEX

T. Denean Sharpley-Whiting is Associate Professor of French and African American Studies and Acting Chair of French at Purdue University — West Lafayette. She is the author of *Frantz Fanon: Conflicts and Feminisms* and coeditor of *Spoils of War: Women of Color, Cultures, and Revolutions* and *Fanon: A Critical Reader*. She is an editorial board member of the *International Journal of Francophone Studies* (U.K.) and coeditor of the journal *Romance Languages Annual*.

Library of Congress Cataloging-in-Publication Data
Sharpley-Whiting, T. Denean.
Black Venus : sexualized savages, primal fears, and primitive narratives in French / T. Denean Sharpley-Whiting.
p.   cm.
Includes bibliographical references, appendix, and index.
ISBN 0-8223-2307-9 (cloth : alk. paper). — ISBN 0-8223-2340-0 (pbk. : alk. paper)
1. French fiction — 19th century — History and criticism.   2. French fiction — 20th century — History and criticism.   3. Women, Black, in literature.   4. Stereotype (Psychology) in literature.   5. Popular culture — France — History — 19th century.   6. Popular culture — France — History — 20th century.   I. Title.
PQ653.S55   1999
940.9'3520396 — dc21   98-37728